THOMAS YOUNG: FORGOTTEN GENIUS

An Annotated Narrative Biography

DANIEL L. KLINE

Library of Congress Prepublication Catalog No. 92-183992
Kline, Daniel L., author
Thomas Young: Forgotten Genius

Book Design and Typography: Emily Marks

Published in the United States
Vidan Press
933 Avondale Avenue
Cincinnati, Ohio 45229

ISBN 0-9635046-0-6

Dedicated to my daughter Emily whose creativity and expertise made this book attractive and to my wife, Vivian, an enthusiastic researcher and an unfailing source of support. I also want to thank Professor John Z. Young and Mr. David Gurney for their helpful encouragement.

CONTENTS

ILLUSTRATIONS

Preface

When I retired after a career in medical teaching, research and administration, I happily turned to an old love, Egyptology, to keep me amused. I was startled one day to read in E. A. Wallis Budge's book, *The Mummy*, that Champollion, the brilliant French linguist, was not the first person to translate Egyptian hieroglyphs. A Dr. Thomas Young had published the first translation of any hieroglyphic names and words several years before in the Encyclopaedia Britannica. Since Budge was the Keeper of Egyptian and Assyrian Antiquities of the British Museum and a highly honored scholar, this was not the claim of a "crank" and I decided I had to learn more about this doctor who lived from 1773 to 1829.

After I had read what is available of Young's diary, correspondence and lecture notes, I felt that I had been in contact with one of the most brilliant, wide-ranging minds that had ever appeared in the Western world, and he was a most human individual along with his genius. There is a speculative game some people like to play in which a figure from the past is chosen to come back to life for a conversation. Thomas Young would be my first choice.

Just imagine asking him questions about modern problems when he, during his lifetime, was 200 years ahead of his contemporaries. He would leap intuitively to the answers to questions in physics, medicine, linguistics, engineering and philosophy that are valid today, even though

Thomas Young: Forgotten Genius

he did not have the knowledge we have today of the atom, Einstein's Theory of Relativity, and the invention of Quantum Mechanics.

Intuitively, he felt wave motion could explain not only sound transmission but light also, and even the structure of matter itself. He was so confident of the truth of his insight he dared to challenge the great Issac Newton, who claimed that light must travel as particles and not as waves, because it does not bend around objects as sound waves do. He designed one of the most inspired experiments in all of science to prove that he was correct. Of course, only a handful of scientists of his day gave up their belief that the great Newton could possibly be wrong.

In proving that light travels as waves, he discovered interference between wave patterns and founded the science of Interferometry. He recognized that this was a method for the precise measurement of very small distances and he measured the wave length of violet light (about 15 millionths of an inch). Our ability to carry out space explorations and to manufacture microchips for computers depends on Interferometry, as does the new field of Holography.

Brilliance in one field might be enough for most geniuses, but Young became an expert in the translation of ancient Greek at age 18, and crowned his linguistic achievements by being the first person to translate and publish any hieroglyphic words years before Champollion, who claimed the credit for breaking the code.

Young's proof that light moves in waves, his discovery of Interferometry, and his pioneer translation of ancient Egyptian hieroglyphics might have earned him two Nobel prizes today, but he also did work which gained him the title "Father of the Physiology of Vision." In addition to the discoveries in this area, he proposed a theory of color vision which, for the first time, suggested the brain may not only receive information, but it processes and integrates the information it receives. This is taken for granted by today's neurophysiologists.

Engineers are taught Young's "Modulus of Elasticity" today. Historically-minded engineers might know that he was the first to introduce the concept of kinetic energy. Life insurance specialists might know that he made early contributions to the application of mortality tables to enable the predictions needed for life insurance policies to be written and some linguists may know he introduced the term Indo-European to show that languages from India to Ireland have a common root. Although specialists in many fields may know of Young's contributions in their areas, they generally do not know that the same man made so many contributions in other areas! He even had the audacity from his studies of how solutions form a meniscus in small tubes, to calculate the size of a molecule of water—the first calculation of the size of a molecule that we know of.

Thomas Young: Forgotten Genius

All of these accomplishments were carried out while he maintained a medical practice and he had no students to assist him nor did he have any expensive apparatus. Unbelievably, he was a gregarious man who loved the theater, the arts and even achieved a small reputation as a gymnast and horseback rider!

As fascinating as I found his achievements to be, I was completely overwhelmed by the depth and audacity and modernity of his philosophical ideas. Almost 200 years ago he put forth ideas that are close to those of the most advanced theoretical physicists today. What conversations he and Stephen Hawking would have had! Young suggested that hard objects like baseball bats or concrete blocks may only be types of energy which exist as waves and are interpreted as hard objects by our senses and our brains. He even thought it possible that an infinite number of universes may exist all around us at the same time. The Infinite Universe theorists who suggested this a few years ago might be startled to know how long ago they were anticipated by this man who had no knowledge of the inside of the atom and the extent of the universe which we now know. He felt that light and electromagnetic waves plus intermolecular forces (such as the forces that combine molecules of water into droplets) might constitute one type of energy and gravity another. Einstein and many brilliant scientists were able to bring intramolecular forces (which Young knew nothing about), plus extramolecular forces into a unified theory but gravity has thus far escaped fitting into a unified theory. How could Young possibly have realized that gravity was a special problem?

As I learned more about Young's amazing accomplishments, I decided that I must try to re-acquaint the world with this remarkable man whose name is known to only a few specialists today.

When I was a student, I was struck by C. P. Snow's description of "Two Cultures"—scientists and non-scientists proceeding in parallel paths with very little crossing over in their interests and knowledge. Some of the scientists I knew were more or less well-read in literature, history, art, etc., but few non-scientists ever read about scientists and their work. The highly specialized vocabulary used by scientists is a foreign language to people who are knowledgeable in other fields. It seemed to me that reading about a polymath like Young whose genius spread over such a wide area of human knowledge might be a stimulus for young and not so young persons to become interested in the world of science if the language were not so technical and the individuals came through as human beings. Hopefully it might not only awaken an interest in science in individuals but might stimulate more women to become doctors and scientists instead of the traditional nurses and technicians.

All of the facts in this biography, such as names and

Thomas Young: Forgotten Genius

dates, are accurate to the best of my knowledge and an effort has been made to portray the characters and their relationships in a fashion that is in agreement with surviving records, correspondence and documents. Since the language used by Young and his contemporaries in their correspondence sounds stuffy and stilted to our ears, I have taken the liberty of inventing conversations which will convey appropriate feelings and give a faithful report of individuals and incidents. Since I had a predominantly American readership in mind, I wish to apologize to British and other readers who may find the informality and the Americanisms of my invented conversations a bit jarring. In addition, I felt it necessary to create some conversations and encounters to try to explain how a 31 year-old genius married a 17 year-old woman, as Young did. I also felt the reader might wonder, as I did, why Young's best friend, Hudson Gurney, married a woman when they were both in their thirties although they had known and liked each other since they were teenagers. In their time, unmarried women at 30 were regarded as spinsters—unattractive and unlikely to find a husband. This was certainly not true of Hudson's Mag as her portrait clearly shows. When the source of material is not clear from the text, references are shown in brackets [ ] and are listed as endnotes at the end of the book. Unidentified quotations have been invented as a narrative device to enliven the biography and to make the principal characters and events more real. I believe these inventions are in keeping with the character of the people in the biography and are consonant with the picture that emerges from their surviving documents.

I have included some of the life and background of Young's lifelong friend, Hudson Gurney, in Young's biography. The wild Gurney household at Earlham and "Mag" who started out as "The Rattish Mag" and ended as the much admired, gracious hostess of her millionaire husband, Hudson Gurney, are an integral part of Young's life.

Young's contribution to the translating of the Rosetta Stone and other Egyptian writing consisted in large part in his discovery of the alphabet. While an impressive feat which enabled Champollion to make a start after 10 years of total lack of progress, it must be kept in mind that this was chiefly useful in translating proper names. It took the genius of Champollion to work out with unbelievable speed the meaning of the ancient texts after the hieroglyphs had been converted to English letters. Champollion's documented shabby treatment of Young may have led Young's supporters to overlook this limitation. In describing the remarkable scientific accomplishments of Young, I have tried to convey a realistic picture of the lives of scientists with their triumphs and failures or disappointments. Scientists and scholars are invariably shown as altruistic people dedicated to the pursuit

Thomas Young: Forgotten Genius

of truth. Unfortunately, some scientists and scholars, like people in all walks of life, can be egotistical, ambitious and even dishonest. Often, science is pictured as the sudden dawning of a new idea but scientists who make new contributions build their theories on the shoulders of previous workers and new ideas come from breaking out of set patterns. Thomas Young, who has been called the Leonardo da Vinci of England was such a man. If better known today, he could serve as a useful role model for future scientists.

A Young Genius is Born

Chapter 1

Thomas and Sarah Young must have realized that something unusual had happened to them when their two year old son (also named Thomas) came to them to ask for help with some of the longer words in their family Bible. He had just learned to walk and the Bible was probably too heavy for him to lift. Thomas, with a little help from his parents, had taught himself to read when most children his age are just beginning to talk!

In every generation, babies are born who range from the brightest to the dullest. In addition, a few of them are so much more talented that they stand in a class by themselves. Mozart, for example, wrote original music when he was three and gave a public concert on the harpsichord when he was only four years old. Thomas Young was one of this rare breed. He was born in 1773 into a Quaker family at a time when Quakers were unpopular and discriminated against for their beliefs and their lifestyle. Refusing to take any oath except for God and distinguished by their plain mode of dress and special use of language, they were recognized and excluded from mainstream life.

It couldn't have been much fun to be a young boy or girl in a Quaker family in the little English village of Milverton where Thomas was born. His parents did not allow dancing or any music in the house except for religious hymns. They

Thomas Young: Forgotten Genius

believed every minute of their day should be spent in some useful activity. And they expected their children to do the same! Many of these Quakers became doctors, lawyers, business men, scientists and important political figures. Apparently there was nothing in their stern religion that forbade the making of money and many of them became rich and influential in English life in spite of their being Quakers. They were against war and slavery and believed we were put on this earth to help others and it must have been hard for a high-spirited boy to be so serious all the time. Fortunately, young Thomas was a natural bookworm and he loved to learn new things. Luckily, his parents realized that he was not an ordinary boy and while he had to behave and dress like a Quaker, they didn't force him into a rigid mold when it came to his education. Instead of spending his whole time memorizing, which was the way most people were educated in those days, he was allowed to learn at his own pace and had lots of free time to try his hand at whatever interested him as long as his parents thought it was useful and not frivolous.

Thomas was the first of ten children. Their home, still standing today on North Street in Milverton (which has changed remarkably little in appearance in 200 years), had only a few rooms so he spent a great deal of his first seven years with his mother's father who lived in the nearby town of Minehead. This was fortunate as his grandfather's library allowed him to explore and read the classics. There were no romances, comics or fiction and before he was 4 years old, he had read the Bible and also a book of hymns.

One day Thomas' grandfather had found out that the boy had just read a long poem called *The Deserted Village* by Oliver Goldsmith. The old man may have thought Thomas was just showing off and didn't really know what he was reading. He asked the boy what he could remember about the poem. The grandfather left a note which has been found among Young's papers which said "this (whole) poem was repeated by Thomas Young to me, with the exception of a word or two, before the age of five." [1] Thomas began studying Latin before he was six and also became a very neat writer. He became so good at making sharp points from the spines of goose feathers that when he was at school, he won a bet that he could write 100 lines in a space one inch by one inch.

When Thomas was seven, his father told him that it was time he received some formal education.

"There is a good Quaker boarding school where I think thee will progress rapidly and they have a fine library," he said, knowing this would attract the boy. Young Thomas knew that Quakers did not send their children to regular schools. The other children would make fun of their drab clothes, round-brimmed hats and their "thees and thous." Most of all they were afraid that their children might drift away from strict Quaker habits if they saw the other students singing, dancing, riding horses for pleasure and behaving in a way the Quakers thought a sinful waste of time.

We can picture him arguing, "Why do I have to go to a school? You know that I'll never give up our good Quaker habits and waste my time like some of the other boys. At the boarding school they'll force me to learn along with the other students and you know how well I have been learning on my own." What he really had in mind, perhaps, but didn't dare to say to his father, was that he wondered what was so terrible about having some fun. Did a boy really have to spend every hour of every day in serious study?

But Young, Sr. was too strong a believer in his way of life to consider raising his children without formal Quaker training and Tom was sent off to the school. He hated every minute of it. Fortunately, his parents were wise and kind enough to let him come home when they realized that Tom knew more than his teacher. Perhaps his father realized that he was dealing with a genius and should not be too rigid with him. In any event, he spent the next couple of years educating himself.

It is hard to believe, but records he kept of what he was learning show that by the age of 13, he could read books in Greek, Latin, Hebrew, Italian and French. A relative of Young's wrote that she took him for a walk in London when he was about ten and he was immediately attracted to stalls which booksellers put out in front of their shops. He picked up a valuable classic book—probably in Latin—and began to examine it. The owner of the shop thought that the quaintly dressed little Quaker boy was only pretending to be interested in the book and said, "If you could but translate to me a page of this valuable book, I'll give it to you." Tom began to read from the book as if it were in English and the astonished man winced but kept his word and gave him the expensive book.

His nose wasn't only in books. He read about science and mathematics and became fascinated with experiments that people were doing with light and electricity and he wanted to see for himself. A neighbor taught him how to use a lathe and lent him a book on optics. With the lathe he made himself a telescope to look at the stars and a microscope to examine plants that he collected when he took walks in the neighborhood. When he didn't understand some of the theories about light because he didn't know enough mathematics, he sat down and taught himself algebra, geometry and calculus. If he came across something he didn't understand, he plugged away at it until he felt that he understood it completely.

There didn't seem to be anything in the world that didn't catch his eye or that he didn't want to try for himself. He loved writing with his hand-carved pens and was proud of his ability to write Greek letters as beautifully as if they were in a printed book. Now he discovered that Persian and Arabic were written with squiggles, curlicues and loops. He practiced writing these strange letters and at the same time, with his photographic memory, learned how to read these languages as easily as a fish learns to swim. This would stand him in good stead years later when he tackled hierogylphs. Somebody lent him a book that contained the Lord's Prayer in 100 languages and he spent hours poring over the book as if it were a jigsaw puzzle that he wanted to solve.

After dinner, his parents went regularly to the homes of Friends where they discussed politics and how they might influence their government to settle problems by peaceful negotiations instead of war. The Quakers were especially interested in freeing the slaves who were worked like animals on the plantations of the South in the United States and in the islands of the West Indies. They thought that the American colonists should have more say about their taxes and their own affairs and they supported the Colonists whose slogan was "no taxation without representation." If the Quakers had been able to change their government's policy, there might never have been a Boston Tea Party or an American revolution and what became the United States might have remained a part of the British Empire! Tom took a keen interest in these worldly affairs.

Tom's genius makes it seem as if he wouldn't be popular

with other young people but he apparently never bragged about his abilities or made others feel inferior. He just did things his own way and was happy to help his brothers and his friends. Most geniuses are talented in just one field, like music or math. His genius was different. He loved puzzles and problems. He spent his life solving unanswered questions and thinking up new ideas in an astounding number of different areas.

Thomas Young: Forgotten Genius

Young's Birthplace, Milverton

Photograph by Vivian Kline

Off to Youngsbury and Hudson Gurney

Chapter 2

One night Thomas, Sr. came back from a meeting bursting with news—and it wasn't politics. A very prominent banker and influential Quaker named David Barclay had decided that his bright 12 year-old grandson should have a proper tutor and he was looking for a person "of good character" about his grandson's age to study with him and be a companion. Since the Quakers were a small group, they kept close contact with each other and Mr. Barclay had heard that Thomas who had just turned 14 was exactly the boy he had in mind to join his grandson, Hudson Gurney.

Thomas Young, Sr. could hardly keep his usual quiet Quaker manner as he told his son about the offer.

"Mr. Barclay is not only a prominent person," he enthused. "He is also a learned man with a great respect for education and knowledge. If you joined Hudson Gurney, you would study with him at Mr. Barclay's country house in Youngsbury which is less than 20 miles from London. Some of the most learned and gifted people in London are often guests at Youngsbury and you'd have the chance to meet them and have them get to know you. It will be a bit difficult for you to be so far from home but we can keep close touch by mail. Don't you agree that this is a chance of a lifetime?"

He looked at his son anxiously, knowing that young

Thomas Young: Forgotten Genius

Thomas had a mind of his own. But he needn't have worried. The boy was thrilled at the opportunity, not only to have a tutor but also to have a new friend with whom he could study. Even though Mr. Barclay was a Quaker, he had many London acquaintances from all levels of society and Thomas would have a chance to break out of the Quaker circle that had surrounded him since birth and get a taste of the outside world.

Probably for the first time in his life, Thomas couldn't keep his mind on his books. All kinds of thoughts raced through his head. Would he like Hudson Gurney and would they become good friends? Could he share with Hudson the secret he had not dared to mention to his parents—the excitement he felt at the thought of dancing with a pretty girl? Did the tutor know enough ancient Greek to help him become a complete expert in this language that fascinated him? Most exciting of all, would he meet great scholars and scientists from nearby Oxford and Cambridge Universities? No wonder he was too excited to get a good night's rest until the day he left sleepy Milverton.

All of his possessions, mostly clothes, books and his precious microscope and telescope were put on the stagecoach. Thomas said goodby to his family and climbed into the coach for the first day's ride to Bristol. The next day they stopped at Oxford where he was able to catch a glimpse of the famous University. The coach then went on to London but Thomas and his two crates of luggage were transferred to the personal coach of Mr. Barclay. Mr. Barclay's coach, unlike the one he had been riding in, was padded and had springs, but he could not have cared less what kind of a coach was taking him to a whole new life.

The pair of horses turned into a path between rows of mighty oak trees and there ahead was Youngsbury Hall, a large country house—almost a castle. As the horses trotted between neatly clipped hedges, he had a chance to see the spacious grounds surrounding the mansion with a profusion of carefully tended flower gardens. It was late summer and many of the flowers had passed their peak but he could see that the chrysanthemums were still out in full bloom.

As the coach pulled up before the imposing entrance, a tall, dark-haired, nice looking boy came running out of the house. It was Hudson Gurney and the two boys quickly unloaded Tom's crates and carried them to the room he would occupy, too excited to wait for help from Mr. Barclay's servants. Tom knew immediately that he liked this clear-eyed young man who made no pretense of superiority or stuffiness even though it was his grandfather's house. They became friends immediately and remained close friends for the rest of their lives.

The next five years of Tom's life could not have worked out better if he had written the script himself. The tutor had not arrived yet, and while they were waiting for him to appear, the boys played and studied together and got to know and like each other more and more. Hudson was bright and eager to learn whatever was put in front of him. He had read only the traditional classics, however, and knew only the beginnings of Latin and Greek (which were languages all good students were supposed to learn in those days). He knew nothing about the new wonders of the world of science that fascinated Tom who, in addition to improving his Latin, Greek and other languages, had read all about Newton's Law of Gravity and his experiments with light. Tom was puzzled that ordinary light from the sun could be broken up into all the colors of the rainbow when it passed through a triangular piece of glass called a prism. "Does that tell us something about what light is and how it travels through space?" he wondered.

A few days later Mr. Barclay called the boys into his study. "I have some disturbing news," he told them. "The tutor has found a permanent position at a school and he wants me to release him from his promise to come here. Of course, I will not stand in his way, but he was an excellent scholar and it will take some time to find a replacement. Until a suitable man is found, you'll have to study on your own. Do you think you can manage that?"

Tom could barely hide his excitement at the thought that he'd be his own teacher and not have to follow somebody else's program. Before he could say anything, Hudson spoke for both of them.

"Grandfather," he said, "I think you know that Tom is far ahead of me in his reading. He could assign books to me and test me to be sure I understand what I've read. You wouldn't mind doing that, would you, Tom?"

"I'd be very happy to fill in, Hudson," he responded, trying to keep a sober, Quaker face in front of Mr. Barclay. "As long as you don't call me Sir."

Mr. Barclay looked at the two boys who couldn't hide how excited they were at the idea and with a solemn face said, "I know you both are good, studious lads and won't take advantage of the situation, but before I can consent to having a 14 year old acting as my grandson's tutor, two things will have to change." Then his eyes began to twinkle as he turned directly to Tom. "I offered to have you join Hudson as a fellow student, not as his teacher. For this extra burden I will pay you five shillings a week. Is that acceptable?"

"Oh, yes," Tom gasped. "I didn't expect any money for what will be a pleasure. All of it will be used to buy books."

"There is a second condition," Mr. Barclay went on, "from now on you are no longer Tom, a boy, but Thomas, a man."

Through the beautiful autumn days, the boys studied in the morning and evening. During the afternoons which were still warm, they played outdoors, climbing trees, throwing stones into the Rib river which was at the foot of the gently sloping fields of Youngsbury and roaming the countryside where Thomas taught Hudson the names of many flowers, plants and insects and showed him how to use the microscope he had made. One afternoon, as they finished exploring the remains of a Roman road which ran across the fields and headed toward London, they took off their gray, broad-brimmed Quaker hats and threw themselves down on a gentle slope in front of the house.

"I guess I shouldn't be saying this," Thomas ventured, "but I always feel good when I take off this hat. Somehow, when I am wearing it and the rest of these gray clothes, I feel as if I"m not supposed to smile or enjoy the fun things in life. But I *do* think having a good time doesn't keep me from working hard."

He looked anxiously at his new friend, knowing that Hudson's grandfather was a strict believer in the Friends' customs and wondering if Hudson would be shocked at his thoughts.

Instead, Hudson warmly agreed with him. "I've felt the same way you do for some time but I was afraid to mention it to you because I know you come from a strict family. It's such a relief to know I don't have to keep my thoughts a secret from you anymore."

As the days passed, Thomas gradually learned that Hudson's parents, especially his mother, felt that the grim way of dressing and odd way of speaking with "thees and thous" embarrassed their children in public. "We can't be a useful part of our community if they either laugh at us or think we believe we are superior to them," she believed.

"You would like my uncle John and his wife," Hudson told Thomas. "They have just recently moved to a new home they call Earlham. They felt that the strict rules of the Society of Friends were too rigid for them. "There they are mixing with Unitarians, Free Thinkers, Roman Catholics and many others in addition to Friends. I have had great times with my cousins, uncle John's children," Hudson went on. "You'd like them. Those girls are lively and full of fun and I am looking forward to visiting them soon."

They didn't talk about it, but they both dreaded the day when a new tutor would be found who, they were sure, would chain them to their desks night and day. Thomas in particular did not look forward to having a teacher tell him what to do. He knew that he learned the most when he was left alone.

But finally the day came. "I have found an excellent young man," Mr. Barclay informed them. "He is a fine scholar and he is not a crusty, dried-up old man. I am sure you will benefit from his instruction." Looking directly at Thomas, he added, "You learn quickly. Very quickly. But you need a more experienced and trained mind to help you organize your knowledge and fill in the gaps that occur when

Thomas Young: Forgotten Genius

a person is self-taught." Thomas, who wasn't the least bit bothered by his gaps, swallowed his thoughts and nodded his agreement silently. "There is one other point I want to make," Mr. Barclay said. "I have been reviewing what you taught my grandson and I would like you to continue teaching him Latin and Greek. I will tell the new man, Mr. Hodgkin, that you must have two hours each day for this purpose and, of course, our arrangement of five shillings a week will continue."

Mr. Hodgkin, the new tutor, was a tall thin, sandy-haired young man with the grave manner of a scholar. He was delighted to be relieved of the chore of teaching Latin and Greek to Hudson so that he could concentrate on the classics which he loved. A tutor was often treated as if he were a servant in those days and Hodgkin was very pleased to be in a household where everyone was treated as an equal.

The first thing Mr. Hodgkin did was to have the boys write a few sentences so that he could see their penmanship. Thomas may have been insulted by such a childish assignment. He took longer than Hudson to write his sentences for he had translated them into 13 languages! It quickly became clear to the tutor that he could only help Thomas by suggesting books to him and discussing them with him. Other than that, he left him to his own devices which was exactly what Thomas wanted.

From time to time Hudson left Youngsbury to spend a

weekend with his cousins at his uncle John's new home, Earlham. Thomas waited impatiently to hear what Hudson had to say about life outside the close circle of Friends. And he wasn't disappointed.

"My aunt Catherine," Hudson told him after one of these visits, "has a fixed rule: Always leave children to judge for themselves." This applied to their behavior, too, and Hudson was fascinated and half frightened at the results. "My cousins are a wild gang," he told Thomas. "It isn't that they behave badly but they do whatever comes into their heads. During my last visit, they locked me into the pantry and wouldn't let me out until I promised to describe cousin Louisa's character with complete honesty. I said she was bold, impudent and acted without any restraint but she would give up a great deal of pleasure if it helped other people and she was generous and open. Louisa said she agreed with most of it."

"My sister, Anna," Hudson went on, "was also there. She has caught some of their eccentric behavior and claims she has invented a way to save good writing paper. When she is writing a letter and reaches the bottom of a page, she turns the paper so that the top and bottom are now the left and right edges and writes across the sentences that are already there. It's true that you can read what she's written but she has to space the lines far apart or they wouldn't be legible. I'd rather write in one direction and keep the lines closer."

Hudson really got animated when he told Thomas about a new arrival at Earlham. She was a young girl about 13 years old named Margaret. They all called her Mag. She had been shipped to the Gurney's by her mother who was a very independent Scotswoman. Mag's mother was very wealthy and had married a man on condition that he use her family name instead of his. After the marriage, he rarely did but they stayed together and had eight children, including Mag and a twin sister. When Mag's twin fell ill and was dying, her mother suddenly decided to send Mag to the Gurney's at Earlham. Mag had arrived at Earlham full of unusual ideas. She was intensely religious and believed that every word in the Bible was true and divinely inspired. For her the Church of England was the only true Church. Hudson's cousin, Richenda, told him that they called her "the rattish Mag" behind her back and that she had a fierce temper. Richenda also reported that Mag was afraid of sweet, harmless cows! Thomas noticed that Hudson had anything but a look of disapproval on his face when he described her. He said it was a shame she was so odd because she was the most beautiful girl he had ever seen. Thomas felt a pang of envy when he listened to his tall, good-looking friend talk about the times with his cousins. He hoped that someday he would also be a part of such worldly fun.

Within the next few years, an incredible stream of

information poured into the mind of the young prodigy. His ability to read and write Greek soon earned him a reputation among Mr. Barclay's friends. Mr. Barclay liked to have scholars around him and he often invited them to dinner and permitted Thomas to mix with the guests after the meal was finished. Most young men would have quietly slipped out of the room because these people were world famous professors and educators whose idea of fun was to discuss and criticize the latest Greek translations of other scholars. Thomas didn't seem to realize he was just a young fellow among such distinguished men. Without showing off but in a matter-of-fact way he joined in the arguments, suggested new ways that a difficult passage might be translated and backed up his opinions with quotations from his vast reading.

One of these guests was Professor Porson from Cambridge University who was considered *the* authority on Greek. One night Porson asked the group, "How would you suppose the Latin ampersand (&) came to be formed?" Young thought it might have come from a combination of two Greek letters, "e" and "r." Porson said that was a good idea because in Early Greek "e" and "r" were written together as "α" and a loop on top would make it &. He was startled that Young knew that already.

The Professor was so impressed from exchanges like this that he began to call on Thomas for his opinion with difficult texts. In an ordinary youngster this could easily have produced an unpleasant case of "swelled head," but Thomas didn't think he was anything special. "There is nothing I've learned that anybody else couldn't if he worked hard at it," he wrote to his younger brother Robert. This inability to see himself as a specially gifted person hurt Thomas throughout his life because he talked way over people's heads without realizing it. Even when it dawned on him that he had trouble communicating his ideas with ordinary people, he wasn't able to change. This made him a poor teacher and lecturer.

When Thomas was 16, he came down with a serious illness which might have turned into tuberculosis, a much feared disease in those days. He survived the illness with the help of his uncle, Dr. Brocklesby, who was so impressed with Thomas' learning and liked him so much as a person that he practically adopted him as a son. During his recovery, Brocklesby had a taste of Thomas' independence (which may have endeared the boy to him) when the patient insisted that he wanted more than the thin soups and mushy dishes they were feeding him. He felt that some fish now and then would be a more balanced diet. Brocklesby said all right to this heretical idea but he thought Thomas' refusal to use sugar was nonsensical. He wrote to Thomas, "Your prudery about abstaining from sugar on account of the Negro trade (it was grown in the West Indies by slaves) is ridiculous. My late friend, Mr. Day, abhorred the base traffic in Negro's lives as much as you but he devoured sugar every day. He decided that not eating sugar was a grand gesture but it will not stop the slavery." Thomas stubbornly did not add sugar to his food until later in life.

Youngsbury, near Ware (1992)

Photograph by Vivian Kline

Chapter 3

After this illness, Dr. Brocklesby offered Thomas the opportunity to live at his house in London during the four winter months when travelling was often difficult and Mr. Barclay's house did not have many visitors.

"You can't pass this up," Hudson pleaded with Thomas. "It's the chance of a lifetime to meet people like Samuel Johnson and the great Edmund Burke. Besides can you picture the libraries in London with rows and rows of books waiting for you?"

"I'm tempted," Thomas admitted, "but I don't want to leave you or Mrs. Barclay who was so wonderful during my illness. It's a hard decision for me."

"We'll miss you, too," Hudson agreed, "but you can't say no to a chance like this. We'll keep in touch and London isn't so far away. I'll be able to see you from time to time."

Reluctantly, Thomas agreed. Once he had moved to Brocklesby's for the winter, he met a great assortment of doctors, politicians, scholars and other famous people. Thomas' father wasn't too happy about Brocklesby's fondness for his son. Thomas, Sr. was a very strict Quaker and he thought that the doctor had gotten too free in his choice of friends and his way of life. He knew that Dr. Brocklesby liked to show off his nephew's achievements to others and he was afraid it might spoil the boy. But Thomas,

Thomas Young: Forgotten Genius

Sr. was also a very practical man and he knew that Dr. Brocklesby, who was rich and influential could be a great help to his son's career. After objecting at first, he gave his permission and Thomas regularly spent four months each year in Brocklesby's house.

When Thomas reached his 19th birthday, he began to think seriously about his future and to discuss his plans with Hudson.

"I thought you would surely become a professor of Greek at Cambridge," Hudson said. "Porson already thinks of you as his successor."

"He has said some flattering things to me along those lines," Thomas replied, "but I really don't wish to spend my life in a dusty university. Besides, I would hate to have to push Greek into the heads of reluctant students when most of them would only be waiting for the class to end so that they could head for the cricket grounds or the nearest alehouse. I feel that I should do something that would be more beneficial to mankind and I've decided to become a doctor. When I'm not taking care of the sick, I could continue my experiments in science."

"And that would please your uncle, too, wouldn't it, Tommy," Hudson teased him. The only person who regularly called him Tommy was Dr. Brocklesby who had developed a deep and affectionate feeling for the young genius. Hudson knew that Brocklesby had recently told

To London and Medical School

Thomas that he had changed his will so that his nephew would never have to work again if he lived modestly. "It would be a loss to mankind if a man with your gifts had to waste time earning a living," Brocklesby had told him.

Thomas grinned back at Hudson. "That certainly isn't my only reason for choosing to become a doctor. But I must confess I thought of that and it did help me to decide. I have a great admiration for my uncle."

So in the fall of 1792 when Thomas was 19, he left Youngsbury and rented a room in London so that he could attend lectures in medical subjects and enroll the following year at St. Bartholomew's Hospital. Today students go to college first and then enter medical school (if their grades are good enough and they can afford the tuition). In Young's day, they simply enrolled at a hospital whenever they thought they were ready. They then sat in on lectures that were given by well-known doctors in their specialties, like Anatomy, Mid-wifery (Obstetrics), Surgery, and so on. After two or three years, they requested an examination and a board of experts was formed to decide if they knew enough to become doctors. After that they became apprentices to a doctor for a few years or started out on their own immediately.

Young attended lectures faithfully, taking careful notes and reading the books recommended by the teachers. But only a part of his mind was on his medical training. His notebooks, which friends of his read after his death, are full of comments in Latin and Greek as well as mathematical calulations and scientific ideas that came to him.

Even before entering medical school he became interested in a problem in vision. Scientists already knew that light is bent as it enters the eye so that an object is focused onto the retina (upside down). When an object is far away, the rays of light are parallel to each other by the time they reach the eye and only have to be bent a little. When an object is near the eye, the rays are spreading out and if the eye didn't bend them a lot, near objects would focus behind the retina and be blurry. Figure 1 shows how the eyes do this.

When we change from looking at far to near objects, the entire eyeball might get longer, so that the rays which are diverging when they enter the eye would focus on the retina instead of behind it. This is the way a camera works. Another possibility is that the outer surface of the eyeball, the cornea, might bend more when objects are near or, finally, a third possibility which was not held by any doctors at that time was that the lens within the eye might become more curved so that rays which were spreading out would get bent more and focus on the retina instead of behind it. Most doctors of Young's time thought the cornea changed or the eyeball got longer. Young made some models with glass lenses and found that the eyeball, which is in a bony socket, could not get long enough to explain how we can see near and far objects equally clearly. He did some pretty brutal experiments on himself by pushing a metal bar against his eyeball so that it couldn't get longer as he looked at near and far objects and found he could still see both of them clearly. He used a new instrument which had just been invented called an optometer and showed that the cornea did not change shape when he looked at near and far objects.

He then went to the library and found that the inventor of the microscope, Leeuwenhoek, had studied eyes and had described fibers inside the lens. Thomas got the eye of an ox from an anatomy dissection class at a nearby hospital and examined the lens with the microscope he had made. Sure enough the fibers were there and they looked enough like small muscles to convince him that there was a mechanism for the lens to change its shape. The lens itself was flexible and its shape could easily become more curved by contraction of the small muscles.

Young was eager to tell Hudson about his lens theory. It was his first important scientific work, but he had to wait until his friend came back from a trip to Paris.

Thomas Young: Forgotten Genius

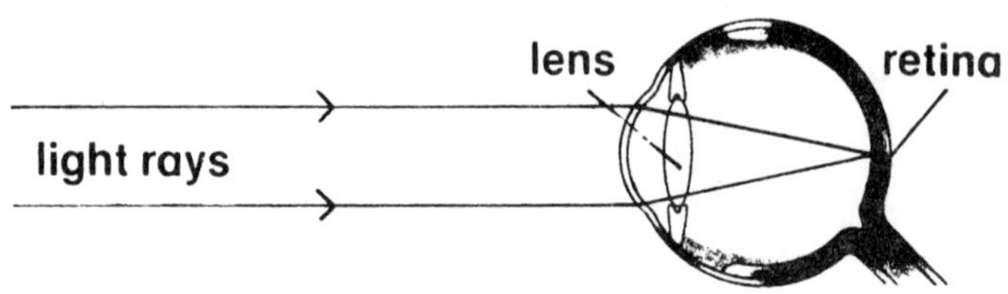

To see objects more than 12 feet,
lens is in relaxed, flattened state.

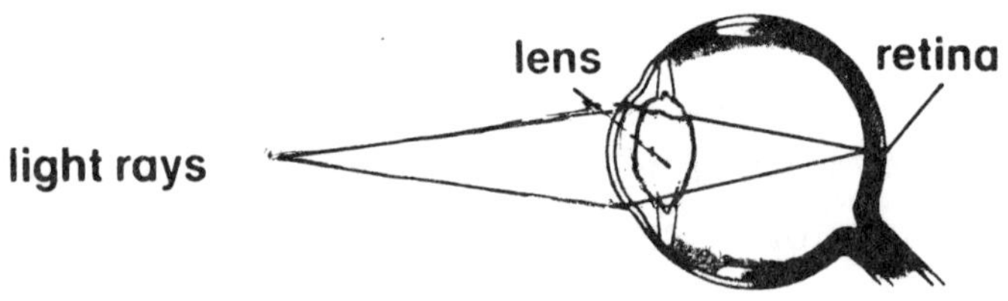

To see nearer objects, lens must bulge to bend
diverging rays onto the retina

Figure 1 How a Lens Adapts for Near Objects

To London and Medical School

It is hard for us to imagine today how Hudson could have gone to Paris when England was at war with France and had been for some years. This was a time when the larger countries such as Russia, Austria, France, Italy and Prussia were grabbing up pieces of other countries (including pieces of each other) and alliances were being made and broken all the time. England avoided most of the fighting but was worried that France would grow too strong and so these two countries fought many skirmishes over the years. At the time that Hudson went to Paris, there was no active fighting going on between them.

A few years earlier, the French citizens of Paris had risen against King Louis XVI and his wife, Marie Antoinette, and had seized control of France. The king and his noblemen had spent enormous sums of money on their homes, their possessions and their entertainment while the poor were forced to pay higher and higher taxes to support the extravagances of the royal family. A story states that when Marie Antoinette was told that the poor had no bread, she is supposed to have replied, "Let them eat cake." Whether the story is true or not, the constant wars and the lavish court life had plunged France into enormous debts and the common people finally revolted. A wave of enthusiasm for democracy and justice swept over France and new laws were passed transferring power from the king to an elected assembly. Americans were particularly impressed because a leader of the revolution was Lafayette who had fought with the Americans in the war against England. Many English people were excited about the revolution in France and wanted to show their support in any way they could. Among them was Hudson Gurney.

Thanks to his father's banking and beer businesses, Hudson in 1793 was now a wealthy 18 year old who was eager to help the French find their way to democracy and the rule of law by following the example of the British. Full of enthusiasm and completely naive about the situation in France, he took his own coach to Dover on the English Channel, placed it on a boat going to Calais in France and once on land, then rode in it triumphantly to Paris. In his pocket was a letter of introduction that Thomas had written for him to a Dr. Marat who had spent a year in London and had found a cure for his own eye ailment which he had described to Young. On returning to Paris, Marat had given up his medical practice and had become the leader of one of the most radical parties in the Assembly.

When the two friends got together shortly after Hudson's return from Paris, Thomas started to tell him about his lens theory but Hudson obviously wanted to talk about his visit to Paris first, and Thomas settled back to hear what had happened that had visibly shaken Hudson to the core.

"As my coach passed the huge guillotine that had severed the head of Louis the XVIth after a hasty trial earlier this year, I shuddered," Hudson began. "Absolute rule must become a thing of the past, I told myself, and some excesses must be expected when people who have suffered greatly cast off their chains. I had no difficulty locating Marat. He is a great hero among the common people of Paris and I presented your letter and arranged to meet with him the next day. In my coach, on the way to the hotel, I had to admit to myself that Marat had frightened me. During our brief greeting, we had been interrupted several times by armed guards. I know enough French to understand that Marat was ordering the arrest of various people without trial. But my education was just beginning.

"The next day Marat and I met again and again we were frequently interrupted by armed citizens. 'Are all of these aristocrats you are jailing enemies of the people?' I asked him. 'Aren't some of them sympathetic with the poor and down-trodden?'"

"Marat's reply astonished and dismayed me. 'Those people are not aristocrats or of the clergy who supported the King,' Marat told me, 'those have all been eliminated already. These are the supporters of Robespierre, that man who started as a believer in democracy now wants to become the dictator of France. He would cut off the head of anybody who is not on his side, and I am one of his enemies because I am against one man rule whether his name is Robespierre or Louis XVI.'

Thomas Young: Forgotten Genius

"At that moment the door burst open and one of Marat's guards rushed in yelling, 'They're here. They're here. Robespierre's thugs are at the front door demanding admission.'

"Marat remained perfectly calm. 'Let them in,' he said to the guards,' and turning to me he added, 'I have nothing to fear from citizen Robespierre. He knows how many followers I have. If he tried to harm me, his head would roll next.'

"Then three men who looked more like beggars than soldiers came into the room. If they were not carrying deadly weapons, they might have been laughable dressed as they were in odd bits of old military costumes. Their leader pointed his bayonet at Marat and said menacingly, 'We know that you are dealing with the English and you are an enemy of the French people. We do not have an order for your arrest today but we have come for the Englishman.'

"The two soldiers came up to me and each grabbed one of my arms. I began to argue with them but Marat yelled, 'Stop!' and the soldiers who were obviously afraid of him let go of my arms. 'This man is an Englishman, yes,' Marat said. 'He has brought me greetings from a fellow doctor in London. Here is his letter,' and Marat showed them your letter. They looked at it but I doubt if they knew how to read. 'He is not a military man and is not a member of the English government. He is here as a friend. His father,'

"

Marat continued in an authoritative voice, 'is one of the most influential men in England. If any harm came to his son, we would soon have the English Navy on our beaches and our revolution would be crushed. Let him go in peace.'

"The three soldiers looked at each other then at Marat and finally turned to me. 'You have your carriage at the door. Get in it and return directly to England,' they spat out. 'If you delay en route, you might yet see our guillotine,' and they marched out of the room.

"Tom, I realized then and there that the citizens had turned against each other. Law and order no longer mattered to them. They were all ambitious for themselves and ruthless toward their rivals."

Young could see that Hudson's brush with the guillotine had left him still shaking at the recollection of the soldiers holding his arms and he realized that in the reign of terror that was now going on in Paris, his friend might have been marched straight to the guillotine.

After a silence, Thomas ventured, "I hope this incident hasn't turned you against the revolution. After all, they have got rid of their horrid king and I hear that land will be re-distributed, the poor can now get justice in the Courts and taxes will be reduced."

"Tom," Hudson replied, "I have seen that people who start with the highest motives can turn into beasts when they get the feel of power. Not only Robespierre, but Marat and other leaders are fighting for control. They have forgotten their ideals and crude ambition is now their driving force. No, I haven't turned against the ideals of the French Revolution but I no longer trust any of the leaders and I will no longer support them."

Then with a sigh, Hudson said, "Enough of my adventures. Tell me what you've been up to, Tom. You had explained your theory to me that the lens changes, not the eyeball. Have you been able to prove it?"

"After your tale of your visit to Paris, my lens theory seems like an anticlimax, but it *is* exciting to me. I have been able to prove, at least to my satisfaction, that it is a change in the shape of the lens that enables us to see near and far objects equally clearly, I am writing my first medical paper on this subject and plan to read it to the Royal Society this winter."

"I am sure the Royal Society will welcome such good work," Hudson said generously. "They are becoming a bit too scientific for my taste, however. I wonder if scholars who are not scientists will find a place for themselves in the Society in the future."

"Don't worry, Hudson," Thomas laughed. "I'm not in it yet and I guarantee that if you continue to publish your excellent Greek and Latin translations, you will become a member before long."

Young wrote his first scientific paper: that the lens and

not the whole eyeball or the cornea changed when we adjust from far to near vision. This paper was read to the Royal Society of London and established him as such a good scientist that he was elected a Fellow in this prestigious Society the very next year. The Royal Society was the most important scientific society in England and he was very young to achieve such an honor. Perhaps the fact that his uncle was one of the Electors may also have helped him to get elected.

The way Young approached his first important scientific contribution is a good example of how a scientist handles a problem, not only then but today as well. First, he picked a question that interested him: how does the eye change from near to far vision? The existing theories that the length of the eyeball or the curvature of the cornea changes did not satisfy him. Then he showed that these theories did not work. Next, with his own theory in mind, he went to the library and read what was known about the lens and satisfied himself with his own experiments that the lens could be the answer. Finally, he proposed a mechanism to explain how the lens could be altered by small muscles it contained. As often happens with new theories, he turned out to be partly right and partly wrong. We now know that the lens is indeed the site of the changes, but the fibers inside the lens are not muscles. The curvature is altered by small muscles which are attached to the outside of the lens. When this fact became known a few years after he had published his theory, he readily gave up the part of his theory that was wrong.

The triumph Young enjoyed at publishing his first scientific paper and having it so well received didn't last, however. The very famous anatomist and physiologist, John Hunter, announced that he had had the idea several years earlier and led people to believe that Young had gotten the idea from him. The secretary of the Royal Society, Sir Charles Blagden, who had a reputation for enjoying gossip, spread the story that he had been at a dinner two years before Young's paper appeared where he had told the group, which included Young, that Hunter believed the lens changed as a person looked from near to far objects.

Young was crushed that anyone could accuse him of plagiarism. He consulted his uncle who had also been at the same dinner.

"I don't have any recollection that Dr. Hunter's experiments ever came up for discussion that night,' Dr. Brocklesby said, "but that was two years ago and people might well believe that an old man's memory should not be trusted, especially when it concerns the reputation of his favorite nephew. Why don't you make a list of all the people who were at the dinner, and you can write to each of them? Let's see, it was at Sir Joshua Reynolds' house and I recall that Boswell and Dr. Johnson were present. Drs. Lawrence and Walker King were also there. You, I and Blagden make eight. Who else was there?"

Between them they recalled all of the ten men who had dined at Sir Joshua Reynold's house that night and Young wrote to each of them, asking if they recalled that Blagden had mentioned Hunter's work. All of them assured Young that Hunter's idea about the lens had not been discussed. Blagden wrote that he couldn't remember exactly what had been discussed that evening even though Young knew he had been spreading the story! Fortunately, the prominent scientists in London did not believe Blagden's rumor but were waiting to hear what Hunter himself would say when he gave a lecture on the eye the next year.

Three months later, Hunter died but Young's troubles didn't stop with Hunter's death. Hunter's practice was taken over by Dr. Home, a distinguished physician. Dr. Home presented a paper on experiments he had done with a well-known eye specialist as his assistant. He said they had tested the vision of a patient whose lens had been removed from one of his eyes because of a cataract. According to them, the patient had no difficulty seeing near and far objects clearly with the eye that had no lens. He said Dr. Young was wrong.

From his own studies, Young could not believe that a person without a lens could adjust to see near and far objects clearly. But what could he do in the face of this statement by two eminent doctors? He retracted his paper but he was

Thomas Young: Forgotten Genius

personally unconvinced.

Young's reputation went into a temporary tailspin because of this bizarre happening and it was not helped when further studies showed that the fibers inside the lens were not muscles. However, during this time, he kept working toward his MD degree and never lost confidence in himself. A person who knew him well said:

"His manners were very quiet and pleasing; (just) like those of the more cultivated members of the Society of Friends to which he outwardly adhered, though he had already abandoned many of the peculiar customs by which they are distinguished. His conversation on classical and scientific subjects show a confidence and precision which are far beyond his years, whilst his ignorance of popular literature and of the habits of thinking of his equals in age and station are in striking contrast with the range and accuracy of his other acquirements." [2]

In other words, Young did not have the faintest idea of what ordinary people were reading and talking about. He probably could not have named any of the cricket stars or knew which were the best teams in England. He *was* aware of this and was beginning to feel uneasy about how much he was missing in the world of ordinary people. From this time onward, he gradually became one of those known as Liberal Quakers who felt that the strict Quaker rules left many innocent pleasures out of life. Why not enjoy light music, dancing, the theater, riding horses for pleasure and other pleasant activities without giving up your interest in helping others and your opposition to war?

During the year that Thomas was taking courses at St. Bartholomew's Hospital, he began to travel around outside of London and, thanks to introductions by his uncle, he was able to stay overnight at the homes of some very famous and important people. He visited Herschel who let him look through a large new telescope that he had just acquired. He also visited Dr. Erasmus Darwin, the grandfather of Charles Darwin, who some years later proposed the theory of evolution, and spent two days with the Duke of Richmond, one of the most powerful men in England and head of Ordnance which supplied guns to the English army and navy. The Duke of Richmond was so taken by the bright young man that he asked him to become his personal secretary. This was the chance of a lifetime for a 21 year old. He discussed the matter with his uncle who said he'd have to decide for himself whether to give up medicine though he clearly didn't think he should. Edmund Burke, a friend of Brocklesby's and one of the most important political figures in all of England, advised him: "Don't tie yourself down but give up medicine and go into law." Naturally, Thomas also asked Hudson what he thought he should do.

"Hudson," he said excitedly, "what an opportunity this

is for a young fellow like me. Do you know what the Duke would pay me? Two hundred pounds a year. Enough for me to live like a prince. And I'd eat at the Duke's table. As you know, he is a well-educated man and his guests are the pick of London society—doctors, lawyers, scientists, educators-they all come there. He promised that I'd have enough time to study. I could use his library and he'd let me build a laboratory. What more could I ask for?"

"Why not say yes?" Hudson asked. "Are there some drawbacks you haven't mentioned?"

"Well, Uncle Brocklesby thinks I shouldn't give up my studies at this time in my life. He is afraid that I'll get used to fancy living and will get so deeply involved in politics that I'll never go back to medicine and forget all my Greek if I stop now. I think I can handle this all right. After a few years with the Duke, I'm sure my interest in languages and science will still be there."

Hudson, who could read his friend very well, knew that something else was bothering Thomas and he made a shrewd guess what it was.

"You can't picture yourself, a Quaker pacifist. working for a man who is in charge of supplying guns to the British Army and Navy, can you?" he asked.

"That is my big problem," Thomas confessed. "You know that I'm not a strict Quaker anymore in some of my habits, but I haven't given up my basic belief that war is evil. However, I've been thinking lately that being a pacifist isn't so simple. There are stories that I'm sure you've heard, Hudson, that a young French officer named Napoleon Bonaparte hopes to become the head of France and he has the ambition to conquer all of Europe including England and make us all a part of a vast French Empire. I understand that he doesn't listen to anything but force and the only way to stop him is with our Army and Navy. One day I feel we must stop him, even if it means war. The next day I know war never settles anything and it would break my mother's heart if I left the Society of Friends. I can solve almost any problem that I tackle, Hudson," he went on, "but this one does not seem to have one good answer."

After much anguished thought, Thomas wrote a gracious letter to the Duke thanking him for his wonderful offer but saying that he couldn't accept it at this point in his life. He just couldn't break with the Society of Friends at this time.

On to Edinburgh

Chapter 4

After a year at St. Bartholemew's, Thomas could have applied to Cambridge University to finish his medical degree work in a year or two. With his grades and recommendations, he would have no trouble getting accepted. However, he chose not to go directly to Cambridge. Instead he decided to go to medical school in Edinburgh, Scotland for a year and then to Gottingen in Germany for a second year. The reason he gave was that these two schools were the best in the world. Cambridge had a fine reputation but he wanted the best. There may have been other reasons that he didn't mention. Cambridge and Oxford were the only schools in England that gave an MD degree at that time. In order to go to either one, however, an applicant had to swear that he was a member of the Church of England. Quakers were called Dissenters and were not admitted. Thomas could have changed his religious affiliation easily but he was not willing to do so just then. It is also possible that he was a little scared of the idea of being a doctor and wanted to put it off for a while. He was never afraid of his ability to treat sick people but he knew that he was too scientific for most patients and did not have a warm bedside manner. Intellectuals liked him. Ordinary people found him polite and courteous but didn't warm up to him. He could have used a few funny stories to put patients at ease but it just wasn't his nature even to try.

Thomas could have gone to Edinburgh by coach, but instead. he bought a horse and laid out a route that would have stop-overs at homes to which he had letters of introduction. For the three hundred mile journey his diary listed what he took along:

"A pair of saddle bags, well-filled with 3 or 4 changes of linen, a waistcoat (vest) and breeches, materials for writing and for drawing, paper, pens, ink, pencils and colors; packing paper and twine for minerals; soap, brushes and a razor; a flute in a bag, some music, bound with some blank music paper, wafers; a box for botanizing; a thermometer; two little bottles with alcohol for preserving insects; a bag for picking up stones; two maps of England and Scotland; letters of recommendation; a pair of shoes; straps and paper for drying plants." Not what most students usually take to medical school!

The horse didn't seem to have any trouble carrying Thomas and his baggage. Traveling alone in those days wasn't completely safe. There were highwaymen who occasionally stopped travellers and made the horse's load much lighter, but he didn't meet any. With his introductions, he was welcomed at many places en route. People were delighted to have a visitor to break up their days and bring the latest news from London. They often put on musicals for his benefit and he joined in with his flute even though he knew he wasn't very good at it. He also joined their dances and wrote to Hudson that some of the young women were very pretty and had pleasant figures. He was just learning all the intricate dances that were popular in those days and among his papers was a sketch showing how he tried to reduce one of the dance steps to mathematics! He must have seemed to be a good catch for some of the young women who would like to marry a bright, talented man from London.

He had a wonderful year in Edinburgh though he spent most of his time with the faculty and didn't mix much with other students except that he boarded with some fellows from England and two Germans. In order to learn to speak and understand German (Thomas could read and write the language) the three English students agreed they would speak only German in their rooms and would have to pay a forfeit if they broke the rule. Unfortunately for Thomas, other students from England kept visiting him and he had to talk to them in English and put money into the pot.

The medical school had excellent lecturers and Thomas learned a lot from them. Anatomy professors, however, had problems in getting cadavers to dissect. The city had promised the school to turn over the bodies of executed criminals and unknown dead paupers who died but the supply was very limited. Because of this problem, Thomas never got to dissect a body. He had to learn which nerves to

Thomas Young: Forgotten Genius

cut and where different organs were located from textbooks and demonstrations that were carried out by the professors at the far end of a long room.

The professor of Greek at Edinburgh had heard of Young's reputation and they spent many evenings together, along with other professors who taught classic literature. Thomas' whole time wasn't spent in study, however. He pretty much threw off all of his Quaker customs and plunged into the enjoyment of things that he felt were innocent pleasures. He went to the theater and took in every play that was offered. One evening, there was a knock on his door and the man standing there in Quaker clothes introduced himself as Mr. Cruikshanks. After politely asking about Young and his family's health, Mr. Cruikshanks said, "I hear you have been at the play, and hoped that I should be able to contradict it."

"I have been several times," Thomas replied calmly. "I think it is right for me to do so. I am sure that you are also determined to discourage my dancing and singing, and I am determined to pay no regard whatsoever to what you say."

In addition to his medical classes, Thomas filled his days from 8 a.m. to 10 p.m. with lessons in flute playing, dancing, gymnastics, horseback riding and theater going. He earned quite a reputation in gymnastics by tricks he did on the stationery horse and by learning to walk a tightrope. In horseback riding, he wrote to a friend that he was able to ride two horses at once with one foot on the back of each!

At the end of the University session, he bought another horse and made his way back to London by a roundabout route which took him first to the northernmost tip of Scotland, John O'Groats. Then he headed south, stopping at places where he had introductions and spending a few days in the lovely Lake District in England where many poets have lived and written.

From his letters, we know that he was charmed by the hospitality of the people he met and by their pretty daughters. At one memorable stop, he arrived in time to join a birthday party at the castle of the Duke of Gordon. Before dinner, they talked and to impress the Duke's three charming daughters, Thomas produced some verses he had written. After dinner, the men had drinks and smoked their cigars while the women began to dance in the ballroom. Thomas never smoked but he had learned to enjoy a sip of sherry. The men then joined the women dancing and he had such a good time that when the oldsters decided it was time for bed, he went on dancing with the young women until midnight. The next day, he was taken on a deer hunt. He couldn't bring himself to shoot at the deer when it had been flushed out by hunting dogs and was happy to see it escape. That morning he had been flattered to discover that one of the Duke's daughters had memorized some of the verses she had asked him for the previous day. As he wrote in his diary,

Thomas Young: Forgotten Genius

"One of the girls was lively and vivacious, the second was pretty and naive and the third one (the one who had recited his and other poetry) was intelligent and interesting."

He seemed to think they were all very attractive. "I almost wish I had broken an arm or a leg to give me an excuse to stay longer, but I had to move on or I would never get to Gottingen." He just wasn't ready to settle down yet.

Thomas returned to London where his uncle was impatiently waiting to hear all about his travels and his year in Edinburgh even though Thomas had written to him several times each week. Brocklesby was delighted that his letters of introduction had given Thomas an entree into so many homes and into the circle of eminent classical scholars in Edinburgh. He hung on every word that Thomas related. After a year's absence, Dr. Brocklesby seemed much older and tired more quickly but his mind was as keen as ever. He had another nephew, Mr. Beeby, who was not at all intellectual and lived in Ireland where he spent his time hunting and fishing and being the country gentleman. Although he liked this nephew also, it was obvious that Brocklesby was reliving his life through young Thomas.

It was now time for Thomas to visit his parents at Milverton. He was eager to see them but was nervous about the reception he feared he would get from his strict father when he showed up in fashionable clothes. He resolved not to duck the issue by wearing Quaker clothes and the only concession he would make was to speak with him as thee and thou which he had done throughout his childhood.

Thomas' father's ambivalence toward his son was apparent as soon as they greeted each other. Thomas, Sr. had been braced for this meeting since young Thomas wrote often from London and Scotland and made it painfully clear that he had adopted the clothes of the circle of highly placed people he had come to know. But actually seeing his son in fashionable breeches, a ruffled scarf and with powdered hair was visibly shocking to him. On the other hand, he loved and had great respect for his brilliant boy and knew that Thomas was embarked on a career that was bound to be worthwhile and highly successful.

After greeting his family, the two men and Thomas' mother moved to the small living room to talk. Thomas' mother took up her knitting needles, settled into a rocking chair and prepared to listen to the men.

"Thee looketh marvelously prosperous," Thomas, Sr. began. I trust thy insides have not changed as much as thy appearance."

"Thou knowest I will never give up the worthy principles thou hast ingrained in me from childhood," Thomas responded firmly. "But, as I have written to thee, I feel that there are many pleasures in life that are not looked on favorably by the Society of Friends and I intend to make them a part of my life. I have taken lessons on the flute, dancing and horseback riding and I enjoy the theater. Dost thou truly see any evil in such innocent pleasures?" He glanced at his mother who was not nearly as strict as her husband and saw that she was smiling as she stitched.

"No," Thomas, Sr. answered honestly. "These activities are not in themselves evil, but they take valuable time from thy serious studies and I fear thou may drift from our ideals."

"Never fear, father," Thomas responded, "I wake up an hour before my fellow students and retire an hour later. I am fortunate to have an excellent memory and my studies have not been neglected."

"Thou art now a man," Thomas. Sr. said with good grace. "I cannot alter what thee and thy uncle have chosen to make of thee and I trust thou wilt always be a credit to thy family and make good use of the unusual talents God has bestowed on thee. Come, let us go to sup, if our plain fare is not distasteful to thee," he added with a sudden smile.

The Quakers did not take every word in the Bible literally and they accepted the new knowledge being discovered by scientists but as far as Young was concerned, no church or Bible was needed to stand between him and God. Thomas didn't feel that this was the right moment to tell his father that he did not feel there was much difference between one church and another. He could follow his own inner beliefs no matter what label people put on him.

Chapter 5

Before leaving for Gottingen, Thomas spent two happy days with Hudson Gurney. He then embarked on a boat for Hamburg, Germany. The voyage across the rough English Channel took six days and he was seasick the whole time. But the boat finally docked and he was greeted by the two students he had known in Edinburgh. They quickly filled his empty stomach with solid German food. After five days in Hamburg, he took the coach to Gottingen. It was a horse-drawn wagon with curtains instead of glass and had no doors. The ride wasn't too bumpy but it took two days to cover less than 30 miles.

The University of Gottingen at that time was considered to be the best in Europe. It had outstanding professors in every branch of learning and one of the largest libraries in the world. Thomas, who had already learned enough medicine at Cambridge and Edinburgh to become a physician, attended many lectures but he also took more lessons in flute playing, horseback riding, dancing and art appreciation. On Saturdays, he went to public concerts to which ladies were admitted free. There was also a party given by the students every Wednesday and on Sundays, professors with their wives and daughters held open house for students to play cards, dance and talk. We don't know if he ever admitted to his father or mother that he had learned to play cards!

In Edinburgh, thanks to letters of introduction from his uncle and other friends. he had been accepted as an equal by the Professors and had enjoyed many evenings at their homes. In Gottingen the Professors rarely invited students to their homes. Thomas wrote to Hudson that he thought this was partly due to the fact that they were paid very poorly and couldn't afford to have students at dinner and partly due to the custom they all followed that a teacher never spoke to a student outside the classroom. A teacher and a student might have had an animated discussion in a classroom but if they passed each other in the street a few minutes later, the teacher walked by as if the student didn't exist. This wasn't just the case in Germany. There is a story that a student at Cambridge got caught in a sudden shower. He took refuge under an archway and discovered that one of his professors had done the same thing. "It's awfully wet out there, isn't it?" he said politely. "Questions by students to faculty should be sent through the Provost's office," the professor replied frostily.

Dr. Brocklesby along with many Englishmen did not like the Germans and was contemptuous of their knowledge. Thomas wrote to him that he didn't think the Germans were smarter than the English but he was impressed that they translated all of the new scholarly and scientific papers that appeared in England as soon as they came out. He thought the English knew only what they themselves were doing but the Germans kept up with the advances in other countries as well as their own. Germany, about 1800, was not a single country but consisted of a number of separate states. Many Englishmen (and French, too) were afraid they would combine to form a powerful country that would be a military threat to the rest of Europe. (This fear actually came to reality about 100 years later.) Thomas felt that a true liberal person should rise above nationalism and, like Socrates when he was asked to what state he was a citizen, should answer, "the World." In his journal, Thomas wrote, "A man who has formed friendships with inhabitants of different parts of the globe will find enough to love and to disapprove of among every people; and perhaps one who has acquired the faculty of communicating his thoughts with equal ease to the individuals of several nations, will find himself as much at home in the one as the other." [3] This is the true Quaker spirit.

At the end of the school year in Gottingen, Thomas applied for an examination to qualify as a physician. Several other students were examined the same day. They studied like mad before the exam—a practice that even then was called grinding—but Thomas didn't bother. He looked forward to the oral exam as a good chance to discuss medicine with learned men. The four examiners were seated round a table which was loaded with cakes, small sandwiches and wine. The questioning, he found was calculated to see how well the students knew their material but the Professors were lenient in accepting the students' answers. He passed with ease.

He also had to present a thesis of his own choosing. He spent a lot of time on it and wrote the entire thesis in Latin. We don't have a copy of it but from others we know that he had invented an alphabet of 47 letters which he claimed could express every sound that a human could make. Therefore, it could serve as the basis for an international language. Of course, nothing was known in those days of the language of a primitive tribe in Africa that speaks in clicks! The idea of a universal language was in line with his belief that if people of various nations could communicate with each other, there would be more understanding and fewer wars.

Thomas had hoped to travel through much of Europe before returning to England but the French were fighting the British, Austrians and Italians at that time and he had to confine his travels to German states. On horseback, hoping he wouldn't meet any French soldiers or displaced persons who were living off the countryside, he visited doctors, literary men, scientists, artists and even went down into a mine to see how it worked.

One unusual character he described in a letter was a Professor Bereiss. Thomas wrote that he was the most vain person he had ever met and pretty much of a fraud. The Professor had 11 collections of various objects which were mostly fakes. He had three robots: a flute player, a fife and drum player and a duck which waddled and digested oats (he claimed). He boasted that he could make all the money he wanted, not by turning metals into gold, but by another process which he wouldn't tell anybody about. He did have an amazing collection of genuine paintings including ones by Raphael, Michelangelo, Correggio, Durer, Holbein, Rubens, and Rembrandt. When Thomas had to leave after five hours, the Professor didn't say he was sorry to see him go but said, "I am sorry for you that you can't stay longer."

When Thomas made his way back to Hamburg, he found that he had to wait two weeks before the wind would be favorable for sailing to England. While he waited, the Governor of a nearby town invited him to join a party he was giving in honor of his own birthday. He wrote in his diary that the Governor had two pretty daughters and an even prettier cousin who was his partner in many of the dances.

Chapter 6

After eight seasick days, he landed in England and stopped in at the Gurney's. He then visited his uncle before making his way to Cambridge where he enrolled for another M.D. degree. When he had gone to Edinburgh and Gottingen, he thought those two years would satisfy his requirements at Cambridge and he would just have to pass their exams. However, while he was away, Cambridge changed its rules and said that a candidate must spend two consecutive years at Cambridge. Regretfully, he settled down for two more years of college that he didn't need. He also had to become a member of the Church of England. By now, he didn't care what label people put on him. He just wanted to be free to become a doctor and to do scientific research. Hudson Gurney wrote in his diary that at the same time Young joined the Church of England, he retained a good deal of his Quaker creed.

In the 18th Century, Cambridge and Oxford Universities had sunk to a low level which was to last until about 1775. An historian wrote, "At both Universities the undergraduates were entirely neglected by the great majority of the Fellows, though here and there a College Tutor zealously performed duties that ought to have been shared by the whole college. Noblemen's sons and rich students were much in evidence, and for whom large allowance was made in matters of discipline and they were often accompanied by tutors of their own. The professors of the University seldom performed any of their supposed functions. No lectures were given by any professor of Modern History at Cambridge between 1725 and 1773; the third and most scandalous holder of that Chair died from a fall while riding drunk from his vicarage." [4] Fortunately for Young, Cambridge had improved greatly by the time he enrolled in 1791.

The Professor of Anatomy at Cambridge had the same problem of obtaining enough cadavers for dissection that Thomas had observed in Edinburgh. Queen Elizabeth I, about two hundred years earlier had given a formal grant to the college of two bodies a year of executed criminals or unknown dead persons. But this was not enough for the needs of the medical school. In desperation, grave robbers were hired to dig up fresh burials. One of the corpses brought in turned out to be that of Laurence Sterne, the famous author of *Tristram Shandy*. There were even rumors that the grave robbers may have helped some people to early graves!

Thomas was a few years older than the other students and he was admitted as a Fellow Commoner. This meant that he ate at the faculty dining table, not with the students. Fellow Commoners wore special gowns trimmed with gold or silver lace and had caps covered with velvet which had tassels of gold and silver. These fancy uniforms were not just for special occasions; they were worn every day. Thomas' college at Cambridge was Emmanuel. The social life of the faculty was more or less run by a group called the Parlour. He was elected president of the Parlour after he had been there only six months which was a real social triumph for a young man who was only a Fellow in the College.

The members of the Parlour made weird bets which had to be paid off in wine. Harwood, the Professor of Anatomy won a bet that he could disguise himself within a week so that another member of the faculty, Blackall, wouldn't recognize him. He dressed up as a bricklayer's helper and Blackall didn't spot him among the bricklayers. Young won several bets which were more scientific. He won a bet that he could calculate the angle that would be made if two points on opposite sides of the earth were to meet on the surface of the sun. He lost a bet that he could produce a new theory of sound. The members of the Parlour ruled that his theory wouldn't work. Later it proved to be true.

Young didn't mix much with the other students. Perhaps he wasn't interested in their activities and preferred to spend his time with the faculty. With a mixture of derision and respect, the students called him "Phenomaenon Young". He never said or did a rude thing but he didn't make any use of the usual polite remarks that were a customary part of people's conversations. He never volunteered his own knowledge but if asked about the most difficult subjects, he answered in a quick, off-hand way and did not act as if he should get any credit for his brilliance.

It is hard to figure out what Young did at Cambridge. He was seldom seen in the libraries and there were no books or papers on his table. He continued to ride horseback at which he had become expert in Germany and loved jumping over the highest fences and hedges on the most spirited horses he could find. He also continued gymnastics and was especially good at vaulting on a stationery wooden horse. He said that the students respected him more for his gymnastics than for being an expert at writing and translating Greek. He seems to have spent most of his time doing scientific experiments and reading the latest publications on sound and light.

In December of his first year at Cambridge, his uncle died. Brocklesby left his lands in Ireland to his other nephew. He left Young his house with all of its contents and enough money so that he could live modestly on its interest without having to earn a living.

Chapter 7

In the spring of 1799, when Young was 26 years old, he left Cambridge, set up an office at 48 Welbeck Street in London, and launched his career as a physician and scientist. Cambridge was still operating under rules that had been set in place 150 years earlier so he was not awarded his M.D. degree from the University until he was 35, but he could practice medicine because of his training at Edinburgh and Gottingen.

Starting his medical practice was easy for Thomas. He had many friends who were wealthy and admired him. He also probably took over some of Uncle Brocklesby's patients. But Young never developed a passion for curing sick people. He became a good doctor at diagnosing their ills and treating them but his real love was for science. It is no surprise that a man with his kind of mind would not find treating the sick fascinating since at that time there was very little doctors could do for sick patients. Mostly, they tried to keep the patient as strong as possible so that he (or she) could cure himself. There were no antibiotics and all the physician could do was to keep the patient in bed, try to get him not to overeat or drink and hope for the best.

There were a few procedures that were tried even though they had no scientific basis and didn't act against any particular disease. One of them was bleeding. It was believed that cutting a vein and letting some blood run out helped to get rid of poisons and stimulated the patient to get better. Some doctors put blood-sucking leeches on the arms and legs of patients. Surprisingly, in addition to surgeons, barbers were also permitted to bleed patients. That is why barber shops until recently had red-striped poles outside their shops. Young thought moderate bleeding might be helpful but he was against taking large amounts of blood as some doctors did. He called them butchers. Another treatment was to give the patients drugs which caused vomiting and diarrhea or to try to sweat the poisons out of people with hot baths. Some of the doctors got so enthusiastic in their bleeding, purging and sweating of the sick that there was a general reaction against them. One witty man wrote a verse which he circulated anonymously around London about a doctor named Lettsom:

> When any sick to me apply
> I physics, bleeds and sweats 'em
> If, after that, they choose to die
> Why verily, I. Lettsom.

The first chemical treatment of a specific disease occurred only five years before Thomas became a physician. Dr. Jenner had noticed that milkmaids who got a disease called cow pox did not get the more dreaded disease, small pox. He showed that the injection of fluid from the sores of a girl who had cow pox into a boy prevented him from coming down with small pox. This was the first vaccination.

In a swing away from "bleed 'em and purge 'em" treatment, seaside bathing became a very popular recommendation for those who could afford it. The most famous seaside resort in England was Brighton and a smart, enterprising man built hotels and rounded up trained nurses so that the town of Worthing also became a fashionable seaside place for the sick, "to be pickled in brine" as someone put it. Young spent 15 successive summers there. He treated wealthy people and some poor patients without charge but, best of all, he had time to read and work at his scientific puzzles.

Young never built up a thriving practice. Patients left him as fast as he found new ones. The general opinion was that he didn't have the right personality to make his patients feel a warm relationship with him and was too matter-of-fact in his manner. It was lucky that Young never built up a busy practice or he might not have had time to carry out the experiments, develop the theories and make new discoveries which have set him apart from all other men.

Young was invited to give a series of lectures at the Middlesex Hospital. He took these lectures very seriously even though he knew his audience had little background in the sciences. To a friend, he wrote:

"I have been spending a month on some chemical investigations merely because I was asked to give these lectures on chemistry and pharmacy. I consider that I should have no right to give lectures on these subjects if I have no personal experience with them. The longer a person lives, the less he gains by reading and the more he forgets what he has read. The only remedy I know is to write and do experiments yourself." [5] He gave six lectures on Physiology, six on chemistry, twenty on the systematic study of diseases and four on drugs used in medicine, such as laudanum for pain. He repeated the lectures the following year but not many doctors attended. The titles of his lectures show that he covered just about every scientific subject that was related to medicine. We get an idea of the wide range of his knowledge and interests when we find he listed the different common occupational diseases of princes, men of the world, men of letters, comedians, artisans, laborers, poor, army, seamen and prisoners.

He organized his lecture notes and published them as an *Introduction to Medical Literature*. This was a guide for all doctors to read or own. Nothing like it had ever before appeared in English. A few doctors had put out collections of medical papers which contained good and bad, new and old material, with no guide for the reader. Young put in only those books, articles and papers that were necessary for every physician. The most important had an asterisk (*); the next had the author's name in CAPITALS; a third group had the names of the authors in *italics*.

A Great Idea—Light Moves in Waves

Chapter 8

Young's first serious scientific publication had been his proof that the eye can see near and far objects clearly by changes in the shape of the lens. At first the reception of this paper was all a young man could ask for: he was elected to the Royal Society. But this warm reception as we have seen was quickly followed by a dose of cold water. Dr. Home, the eminent physician, had said that patients who had no lenses in their eyes had perfect near and far vision. Although he was sure that Dr. Home could not be correct, Young, with no proof to contradict him, had had to publicly withdraw his claim.

This episode was Young's initiation into the wide world that existed beyond his Quaker circle. It was his first exposure to the reality that although most scientists are reasonably honest, there are a few ambitious, envious and just plain dishonest people among learned scientists and physicians just as there are in all walks of life. His belief that all educated people were honest and generous and were only interested in truth and the advancement of knowledge was severely shaken. He gradually learned that as a genius he stood out among his fellow men and was a target for many who envied him. Unfortunately, Young had no talent for publicity or perhaps he just didn't care enough to insist on credit for his great discoveries. His work was known only among a small group of professors and scientists who appreciated its value. He didn't hesitate to write papers in which he tried to set the scientific record straight but he did not insist on personal recognition. He acted as if he had enough inner pride to sustain himself and did not have so much vanity that he required public acclaim.

During the two years Young had been at Cambridge waiting to qualify for his M.D. degree, he was excused from all classes because he had already taken enough medical courses at Edinburgh and Gottingen. It was as if he had a sabbatical from school and he spent much of his free time studying sound and light. Of course, he had to pass a final examination covering all of medicine.

A friend who had dropped into his room at Cambridge found Young blowing smoke through a long glass tube. The young scientist then plucked the strings of violins and made other noises such as footsteps on the floor and could see by the effect on the smoke in the tube what kinds of waves were set up by various sounds. Although he presented some papers to the Royal Society about this work, what is more important is that it gave him the idea that not only does sound travel in waves but light also does.

This wasn't an original idea of Young's. Throughout history, starting with the Greeks, some scientists have argued that light consisted of particles which move in a straight line while others thought it moved as waves. About 150 years before Young began his experiments with light, Isaac Newton published his theory of gravity. We hear stories today about how he was sitting under an apple tree when one fell to the ground—in some versions of the story it hit him on the head—and he said, "Aha, I have discovered gravity." Actually, he made his great discovery as so often happens in science, by asking a very simple question that hadn't occurred to anyone else. Why don't the planets that circle the sun, fly off into space? A stone at the end of a string flies off if it is whirled around a person's head and the string breaks. There must be a force, he decided, like the string, which keeps the planets circling the sun. This theory, which Newton worked out in mathematic detail so that the orbits of the planets and the timing of eclipses could be calculated, placed him head and shoulders above all the scientists of his day. Later, he turned his attention to light and his book, *Opticks* became the bible for all scientists who studied light. What Newton said, people believed, even if they didn't understand it.

Newton was convinced that light travels as particles, not as waves. It was known that sound moved in a wave-like manner and Newton pointed out that when sound met an obstacle such as a tree, it was not cut off but could be heard behind it. Light on the other hand traveled in a straight line and was cut off by an obstacle. Behind a tree, there was only a shadow. He argued that this was true even for vast distances. During the eclipse of the sun by the moon, the shadow of the moon on the earth has a sharp edge. This argument convinced the scientific world that light does not move in waves and there didn't see to be any need for an alternative theory.

A Dutch physicist named Huygens studied shadows and found that the edges are not sharp but are fuzzy. He also looked at colors which are produced when light is reflected from a thin layer of oil. (You may have seen this if you ever spilled oil or gasoline on a sidewalk.) He concluded that his observations could best be explained if light travels in waves but he didn't offer the strong evidence that would be needed to overthrow Newton's theory.

Young knew that his wave theory would answer many more questions and provide newer insights than Newton's particle theory. Ever since he had read Newton's book on optics, Young had been fascinated by light. What is light? Does it move as particles or as waves? Does it require a medium to travel in? Why does a prism split daylight into many colors? Such questions were often on his mind. He knew that the answers, if he ever found them, would completely change the way we look at the world. Young's intuition and some experiments he had tried convinced him that the great Newton was wrong and that light *does* travel in waves. But how could light move as a wave and yet not bend around objects as sound waves do? He looked for an answer that would get around Newton's objection and one day in a flash of insight, the answer came to him. This inspiration was possible because the vast distances that astronomers were discovering, the tiny molecules that biologists were writing about and the tremendous speeds found in nature were very real to him while his contemporaries still thought in terms of the world they could see around them. For them, the fastest movement of man or animal they had ever seen on the earth was a runaway horse! Here is where Young, with the flexibility of mind and the quiet confidence of a genius, stepped in.

A theory is often abandoned even though we can't show that it is wrong. We can't prove that angels and devils are not flying around our heads and affecting our lives but most people have given up this idea because better explanations have come along. The new explanations based on scientific ideas lead to greater understanding and more applications to our world.

Everyone knew that sound travels about five miles per second because people could roughly tell how many miles away a flash of lightning had occurred by counting slowly until they heard the sound of thunder. It was also known that sound spreads out from a source in waves that vary from inches to many feet depending on whether the sound is high pitched or low. Young knew that the size of the waves from crest to crest was related to the speed with which the wave was moving and he knew that light moves enormously faster than sound. Is it possible, he wondered, that light waves are not inches or feet in length from crest to crest like sound waves but are very, very small so that the waves can only reach a short distance around an obstacle?

How did Young know that light moves at an enormous speed? For a long time people thought that light from the sun reached us instantaneously. Almost exactly 100 years before Young was born, however, a Danish astronomer named Roemer actually measured the speed of light with surprising accuracy. How did he do such a difficult thing when light travels so fast and he had such poor instruments in 1675?

For purposes of navigation, sailors had observed an eclipse of the innermost moon of Jupiter which occurs every 42.5 hours. They had tables that showed exactly when this occurred throughout the year in Paris and at various distances from Paris. All the navigator had to know was the time an eclipse would be visible in Paris and how many seconds later (or earlier) the eclipse was observed from his ship and the tables would tell him how many miles he was from Paris. Astronomers knew that the eclipses did not always occur in Paris exactly at the time predicted by their calculations but they couldn't explain the differences. Roemer noticed that the best agreement with the calculated times occurred when the earth's orbit was closest to Jupiter and the worst agreement was found to be when the earth was furthest from Jupiter. He reasoned that the difference was due to the time it took for light to travel the extra distance. The discrepancy was about 16 minutes (roughly, 1,000 seconds) and the distance was about 186,000,000 miles. Even though knowledge of the earth's orbit was inexact at that time and the eclipse observations were crude, Roemer had shown that light does have a finite speed and his value of 192,000 miles per second is not far from today's value of about 186,000 miles per second.

The astronomers were trying to help sailors know where their ships were at sea and Roemer, a curious and informed man, discovered something entirely unexpected from the eclipses of Jupiter's moon. Roemer's remarkable accomplishment is an example of serendipity. That is, a chance discovery by someone who is looking for something else. These lucky chances probably occur to many people but only a prepared mind notices and makes use of them.

Young knew that his idea that light travels in waves would shake the world of science if he could prove it. Could he think of an experiment that would demonstrate conclusively that he was right and Newton was wrong? He could and did, but not before he got into a dispute that was to affect his whole life.

Chapter 9

Hudson Gurney had no money problems. His father was a successful banker and also owned a brewery, so he decided to enter politics because he had strong feelings about some of the government's policies. He had made a small reputation translating Greek and Latin poetry into English, but he wanted to do something more substantial for the public good. In order to get nominated from a district where he was sure to win a seat in the House of Commons, (in England you can run for office from any district—you don't have to live there), he began to call on influential politicians in London and, of course, he took the opportunity to see Young whenever he came to town. One day, he called on his old friend and it was obvious that he had more than politics on his mind.

After a pleasant dinner they settled into overstuffed chairs in the drawing room. Thomas could see that Hudson was agitated by something and he waited to hear what it was as they sipped their after-dinner sherry.

"Ever since I had that close escape in Paris," Hudson began, "I've come to distrust the French more and more. Recently, I've been hearing about Napoleon's grandiose plan to conquer England as well as the rest of Europe. I am convinced that he can be stopped only by force and so several weeks ago I made a contribution to a military fund dedicated to the defeat of that madman. Word of this donation seems to have spread rapidly—look at this." He handed Thomas a letter from the Society of Friends informing him that because of his support of military action, the members had voted that he could no longer call himself a member of the Society.

"Does this really bother you?" Thomas asked. "You and I have given up so many of our Quaker habits that I'm no longer sure what we should call ourselves."

"I'm not concerned about myself," Hudson answered, "but this news will greatly distress Grandfather Barclay and he did so much for me at Youngsbury, including bringing us together. I was afraid this might happen when the Friends learned of my action, but after consulting my conscience, I felt I had to make the contribution. In any event," he added with a half-smile, "this should please pretty Mag at Earlham. That girl is Church of England through and through."

Hudson then took a deep breath and introduced a second subject that was on his mind.

"Tom," he said in his most serious manner, "I've just read your review of Dr. Smith's book on Harmonics. Was it necessary for you to attack him so severely?"

"You know that I never attack an author personally," Young responded. "I simply cannot pretend that a book is worthwhile when the science is so poor."

"I know that's true, Tom," Hudson went on, "but is that

the proper way to write about a man who is admired by so many of the intelligent people of London? You realize, I'm sure, that Smith is the Professor of Astronomy at Cambridge and he has several books to his credit which have been translated into many European languages." At this point, Hudson pulled a paper out of his pocket on which he had jotted down a part of Young's review:

"Dr. Smith has written a large and obscure volume, which leaves the subject where he found it," he read. "These are your words, Tom," he said, "Do you want to make enemies of half of London? You may know that Professor Robison is upset and is preparing a statement that will accuse you—in polite words of course—of getting too big for your hat. There are a number of people who envy you your talent and would be happy to see you taken down a peg by such an eminent man."

Young felt anger rising in him as he always did when he was criticized but he knew Hudson too well to lose control of himself.

"Perhaps you are right," he admitted grudgingly. "I did get a bit sarcastic because I hate to see such a poor effort when he should have known better. It is not a good book and if you are suggesting that I should have pretended to admire it just because the author is famous, I am afraid my tutoring has not stayed with you since you've decided to become a politician."

Thomas Young: Forgotten Genius

The two men looked at each other and Hudson said nothing. He knew that Tom had tried to sting him because he had hurt his sensitive friend's feelings.

"I wouldn't have said anything if this had been an isolated instance," Gurney finally resumed after a pause and a sip of sherry, "but last year you slashed to pieces a paper by Lord Brougham and he is not a man anyone wants to tangle with."

"When it is a matter of mathematics, Brougham is a fool," Young responded hotly. "He knows nothing and only pretends to be a mathematician. I gave his paper exactly what it deserved."

"Look, Tom," Hudson said patiently, "you did not stop with criticism of his work. You tried to make him look foolish. Perhaps he is, but it is not typical of you to lose control of yourself."

Young went to a table, picked up a sheet of paper and said, "Here is a copy of what I wrote: 'When we see an author exerting all of his ingenuity....to oblige us to toil through immense volumes without a small diagram,...we may observe that such an author appears to be confused in his conception of the most elementary doctrines.... He may very well easily fancy that he has made discoveries, when the same facts have been known and forgotten long before he existed. An instance of this has lately occurred to a young gentleman in Edinburgh, a man who certainly promises, in the course of time, to add considerably to our knowledge of the laws of Nature.'"

"Well, Hudson, don't you agree that I was being kind to a man who had written a worthless paper to answer a problem that the Greeks had solved two thousand years ago?"

Lord Brougham is an influential man with many friends," Hudson said. "This could be fatal to your future. You sound like a wise elderly statesman giving advice to a young boy. That's not typical of you, Tom. We have been close for so long that I have a feeling something is bothering you and you are letting out your irritation in your writing. Can I make a guess what it is?" Hudson asked sympathetically. "I believe you are unhappy about the way your medical practice is going. Isn't that true?"

"Well," Young admitted, "I cannot get my patients to come back for treatment as easily as they come back for your father's beer. I can manage without their money but I cannot tolerate the thought that I might be a failure as a physician. I believe that anyone can master any problem if he works hard enough at it."

"That's it exactly," Hudson broke in. "Have you really tried to be a complete physician? You have more talent than any ten men I know but have you been able to become the complete doctor that many people need? One who will comfort them and take care of their needs as individuals and not just treat their illnesses? You know that your heart and soul is in your scientific work. I think you must learn to accept that even you cannot be good at everything. Your friends love you whether or not you are a success as a physician. Perhaps they love you even more to know that you are human. You are becoming a great scientist. Can't you accept yourself as you are?"

They sat in silence for several minutes. Then Young smiled at Hudson. "You are my best friend," he said. "Only a good friend could understand me as you do. You have brought me back to earth. Thanks to you, my irritable mood is gone."

The Great Idea is Announced

Chapter 10

One evening, when Hudson stopped by on one of his visits to London, Young told him he could prove that Newton was wrong—light travels in waves, not as particles. Although Hudson had only the foggiest notion of science, he knew that Young had to have someone to explain his ideas to, and after interrupting his friend to have a large glass of ale brought in, he settled back to hear how Tom was planning to attack Sir Isaac Newton and his followers.

"I don't know much about science," Hudson cautioned him, "but I do know that if you challenge the great Sir Isaac Newton, you'd better have excellent reasons and the hide of an elephant. You will be attacked by the world's most famous scientists. I know that you never pay attention to how others feel about your new ideas. Tom, are you prepared to take on the entire scientific community?"

Young looked at his friend for a moment, then said seriously, "I think this is the most important idea that I have ever had and perhaps the greatest I shall ever have. If Newton were alive today, I am certain he would be urging me to go forward. All good scientists know that their theories may be replaced one day by even better theories that explain more than the old ones. "Yes, Hudson," he went on, "I know I will not be treated kindly by the older men who don't want one of their heroes supplanted but I must go

Thomas Young: Forgotten Genius

ahead. I have some new experiments which makes me more sure than ever that I am right and I cannot suppress it just out of fear of the consequences to my reputation. Until my most recent work, only my intuition and a few observations with thin layers of air between glass plates made me think that light, like sound, must travel in waves. For the past few weeks, I have been studying the effect of temperature on the formation of dew and purely by chance I made some observations that I believe can only be explained by waves, not by particles.

"To observe the dewdrops, I placed a candle in a darkened room and had its light pass through a mist of water. I looked at the images of the droplets as they appeared on a white screen. What I saw were colored rings. The centers were white, then there was a red circle. Around this was a circle of bluish green, then another red circle for each droplet. I noticed that when the drops were smaller. the colored circles were larger. I placed some powders of known size into the light path and measured the distance between the red and the green circles made as the light passed through the suspension of powders. I was able to make a scale that told me the size of very fine powders and I could even measure the thickness of a cob web. I placed a drop of blood between two small pieces of glass and from the colored circles on the screen, I could calculate that the red blood corpuscles averaged 0.0072 mm in diameter." (The best measurements today give almost the identical value.) "Let me snip one of your hairs and with my device I will be able to tell you how thick it is. I do not see how particles could possibly form circles of color but my calculations show that waves could do so when they overlap."

Before leaving, Hudson reminded him, "I hope you remember the talk we had a few weeks ago. "I agree that your wave theory is a tremendously important idea but if you want others to accept it, you must be careful how you phrase your criticism of Isaac Newton. I am still concerned that you have some enemies who would like nothing better than a chance to make you eat humble pie."

"Don't worry, my good friend," Young laughed. "I am now preparing a Bakerian Lecture for the Royal Society. This will be the perfect forum to bring my wave theory before the educated public and it will please you to know how much respect I shall show for Isaac Newton and how gently I shall disagree with him. As a matter of fact, he himself did not rule out the wave theory as a possibility but he was convinced by straight-edged shadows that light could not travel in waves. My respect for him is unbounded and you may be sure I will make this clear to my audience."

Young had begun studying dewdrops and ended up with a method for measuring the size of tiny objects. Not only did Young make use of this chance observation of the colored circles to measure very small objects and distances, but he also was smart enough to realize that this experiment provided evidence that light travels in waves. Like Roemer, who made use of the observations of Jupiter's moons to measure the speed of light, a lucky event that we called serendipity, Young, too, used his observations of the formation of dew to revolutionize the worlds of physics and engineering.

Static from Scotland and the "Young Experiment"

Chapter 11

Young's lecture "On the Undulatory Nature of Light" was given in 1801. His picture of how this brilliant idea came to him which transformed the physics of light is described in a letter he sent to the Edinburgh Review:

"It was in May, 1801, that I discovered, by reflecting on the beautiful experiments of Newton, a law which appears to me to account for a greater variety of interesting phenomena than any other optical principle that has yet been made known. Suppose a number of equal waves of water to move upon the surface of a stagnant lake, with a certain constant velocity, and to enter a narrow channel leading out of the lake; suppose then another similar cause to have excited another equal series of waves, which arrive at the same time with the first. Neither series of waves will destroy the other, but their efforts will be combined: if they enter the channel in such a manner that the elevations of one series coincide with those of the other, they must together produce a series of greater joint elevations; but if the elevations of one series are so situated as to correspond to the depressions of the other, they must exactly fill up those depressions, and the surface of the water must remain smooth. Now I maintain that similar effects take place whenever two portions of light are thus mixed; and this I call the general law of the interference of light."

Thomas Young: Forgotten Genius

Young's lecture aroused so much interest among the members of the Royal Society that he was asked to expand his ideas in a second lecture. As Gurney had feared, however, a number of influential Londoners had turned against Young because of his sharp criticism of Dr. Smith's book. This reaction might have died quietly with no harmful effect on Young or his work if he had not also criticized the paper by Henry Brougham of Edinburgh who never forgave him for doing so.

Henry Brougham had a brilliant mind but he didn't know what to do with it. He had entered high school at the age of seven and quickly became recognized as the brightest boy in the school. He decided to become a mathematician and physicist but soon decided that wasn't for him and he went to law school. He claimed he had been born into an aristocratic family although he was actually the son of a minister and Lord Brougham, as he called himself, was a much admired man about town. He was witty and good company and he moved easily in the world of high society. When he was 18, he dressed and acted in a manner that ensured that he would attract attention. He kept his dark hair cropped short and wore black spats, a black scarf and a black cloak. The people of Edinburgh were fascinated and amused by his knowledge and intelligence, his originality and at the same time his eccentric and humorous behavior. Although he never published any scientific or scholarly work of importance, he made a place for himself in Edinburgh, and later, London society. [6]

After Young had scornfully dismissed Brougham's poor paper, Lord Brougham waited for a chance to strike back. He was one of the founders and an important contributor to a new magazine called the *Edinburgh Review* whose writers were famous scientists, literary authorities and artists. The magazine aimed at a higher standard of merit in literature, art, science and politics than was to be found in other journals at that time and was received by influential men with great enthusiasm. Through this *Review*, Brougham had a chance to launch an attack on Young.

Under a pseudonym, Brougham published an article in the *Review* in which he severely attacked Young and his wave theory of light. He did not offer any substantial arguments against it but criticized Young personally as a careless, uninformed scientist and claimed his work had no merit and should not be taken seriously. Pulling no punches, Brougham wrote (in part): "This paper contains nothing which deserves the name of either experiment or discovery.... It is, in fact, destitute of every species of merit." Going on to say that Young's idea was a smoke screen to hide his ignorance, Brougham wrote: "We wish to raise our feeble voice against the innovations that can have no other effect than to check the progress of Science and renew all those wild phantoms of the imagination which

Thomas Young: Forgotten Genius

Bacon and Newton put to flight..." [7]

Gurney, who was far more worldly than Young, was appalled when he read the anonymous attack. He hurried to London with a copy under his arm to see what his friend's response would be.

"I don't know who wrote this terrible set of lies about you," Hudson said as soon as Young assured him that he had read the article, "but you must not let his nonsense go unanswered."

"The man who wrote the article is Lord Brougham," Young responded. "His style and his ignorance of science are unmistakable. But I have in mind a better answer to his charges than to engage in a battle of empty words with him. I have carried out some new experiments which prove without a doubt that light must travel in waves. In my second Lecture on Light which I am preparing for delivery to the Royal Society, I shall explain the new experiments and answer Lord Brougham once and for all. We have an hour before dinner and it will still be light for a while. Come, I shall show you my new experiments," and he led Hudson to a large room he used as a laboratory.

When they first entered the room and closed the door, Hudson couldn't see anything because all of the windows were covered with dark curtains.

"You'll begin to see better in a few minutes," Young said cheerfully. "I don't know how the eye adapts to darkness. I know the pupils get larger but there must be other changes, too. I hope some day to be able to explain it. I am afraid these experiments require darkness."

Then Hudson saw that a small hole had been cut in one of the curtains so that a circle of light came into the room.

"I have constructed some equipment," Young explained," so that I can place a small screen directly in the path of the light beam and a second, larger screen exactly 15 feet beyond the first one. Now I shall slide the smaller screen until some light passes through two very small slits which I have made in the screen only ¼ inch apart. Can you see what appears on the large screen?"

"I don't understand," Hudson answered him. "There are only two slits but I see many stripes on the far screen. They are black and white. What is happening?"

Young walked to the far screen and pointed to a bright vertical bar. "This is exactly in line with the midpoint between the two slits. According to Newton, this spot should be in shadow but it is very bright. The reason it's so bright is that the light waves from the two slits travel exactly the same distance to reach this point. The crests of two waves reinforce each other. Next to the bright vertical line, is a dark bar. At this point, the light from one slit is exactly ½ a wave length different from the light from the second slit. The crest of one meets the trough of the other and they cancel each other. If you look carefully, Hudson, you'll see

Thomas Young: Forgotten Genius

a number of these stripes on either side of the center bright line. Particles could not produce such a pattern but the interference of waves with each other explains it perfectly.

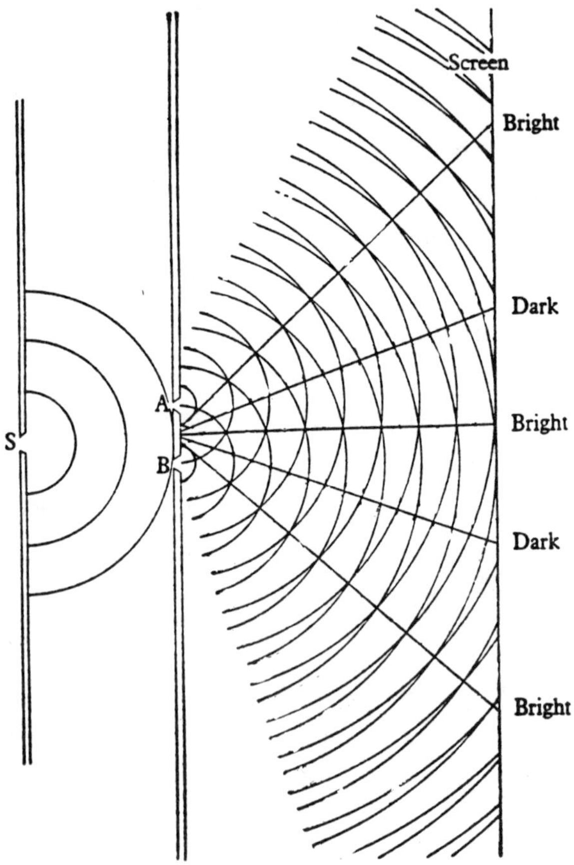

Interference: "Young's Double-slit Experiment"

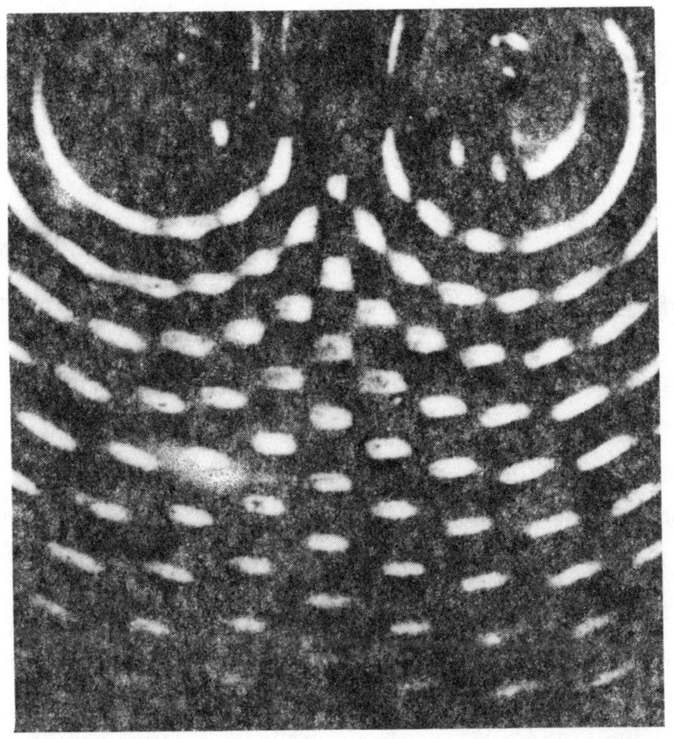

Interference Fringes

Thomas Young: Forgotten Genius

Interferometry, as Young's discovery has been named, has proved to be one of the most useful discoveries ever made. It is the best way to measure exceedingly tiny distances. With the use of lasers which supply a very narrow, uniform beam of light, it is now possible to measure accurately distances less than 1/100 millionth of an inch. Interferometry is the backbone of high precision measurements in tool making, astronomical observations, and was used to measure the speed of light accurately. Without interferometry, high-precision equipment such as computer chips could not be made and we would not have a space program. The new science of holography in which an image of an object can be projected in space and looks so real that you can't believe the thing itself isn't there until you put your hand through it, is based on interferometry. Interference between light waves forms the holograph. If Nobel Prizes existed in Young's day, he might have won the award for his discovery of interference patterns. He certainly recognized their value immediately and used them to measure the wave length of light.

"I've modified this experiment a bit so I can explain why light, even though it moves as a wave, cannot ordinarily be seen behind objects. The bright line you just saw where there should have been shadow according to Newton's theory, was visible only because I created this special circumstance of two slits close together and a second screen a distance away to magnify the effect. I will now place a glass prism in the circle of light coming through the hole I've cut in the window curtain. As you can see, all of the colors of the spectrum are now visible on the near screen with the two slits. I carefully slide the screen until only violet light is passing through the slits. What do you see now, Hudson?"

"In place of the bright, white and dark bars, I see brilliant violet stripes with black lines between them. From what you told me a minute ago, I guess the brilliant violet means that crests of waves of violet light are reinforcing each other and in the black areas a crest is being canceled by a trough. Is that correct?"

"You have it exactly right!" Young exclaimed. "The wave nature of light can no longer be denied. I have also used this experiment with violet light to explain why we do not ordinarily see light behind an obstacle," he went on. "I know that you haven't much use for mathematics except in your business and you're probably beginning to get hungry, so I'll omit the details even though they are not complicated. I can calculate the length of a single light wave from one crest to the next because I know the distance between the slits, the distance from the central violet line to one of the dark ones, the distance betweens the two screens and the speed of light. If you will accept my calculations, they show that each wave of violet light is only .000015 inches from crest to crest. Each wave is like a step that a person takes and the waves are so small that a truly enormous number of them must be formed each second because we know that light travels about 190,000 miles in a second. I have calculated that violet light forms 50,000,000,000,000 waves a second. This means that the height of each vibration (now known as the amplitude) is exceedingly small. No wonder it cannot go around corners as sound waves can. You remember, Hudson, how, at Youngsbury, we estimated the distance from a lightning flash because the sound of its thunder traveled about 5 miles each second? Light travels about 40,000 times faster. Sound waves can be inches or feet from crest to crest but light waves are minute fractions of an inch and vibrate so rapidly that they can only bend around an obstacle slightly."

Before leaving that night, Gurney extracted a promise from Young that he would have copies of his talk made and send them to various people but he could not get his friend to agree to send them to public figures or newspapers.

"Of course I'll send copies of my second lecture to my friends here in London and scientists in Scotland, France, Italy and to several German states." Young promised, "but I do not believe scientists should communicate their ideas through the newspapers. When the true scientists read about my latest experiments, I am certain my theory will be accepted no matter what Lord Brougham may choose to write."

But Gurney's worries were justified. Brougham followed his first attack on Young with one that was even more vitriolic. He wrote in the *Edinburgh Review* that the stripes were caused by particles bouncing off the edges of the slits (ignoring the fact that they were alternately bright and dark) and once again accused Young of careless work. His article dripped with venom and was sarcastic to a degree that was rare when addressed to a Fellow of the Royal Society. After some completely invented criticisms of Young's experimental technique, Brougham added:

"We may now dismiss for the present, the feeble lucubrations [wild inventions] of this author, in which we have searched without success for some traces of learning, acuteness or ingenuity, that might compensate [for] his evident deficiency in the powers of solid thinking, calm and patient investigation, and successful development of the laws of Nature by steady and modest observation of her operations. Has the Royal Society degraded its publications into bulletins of fashionable theories for the ladies of the Royal Institution? Let the Professor [Thomas Young] continue to amuse his audience with an endless variety of such harmless trifles, but in the name of Science, let them not find admittance into the venerable repository which contains the names of Newton, Boyle, Cavendish and...Herschel." [8] What fun Brougham must have had

Thomas Young: Forgotten Genius

showing this latest bit of impudence to his adoring friends.

The non-scientists who formed the overwhelming majority of the *Edinburgh Review*'s readers, accepted Brougham's opinion and ignored Young's work. Young addressed an open letter to Brougham inviting him to do the experiments himself but Lord Brougham was too busy being the social darling of Edinburgh.

Young never did anything to gain publicity for his work outside the small group of scientists who would take the trouble to attend his lectures or read his papers. He *did* want recognition but thought that such recognition would come automatically from fellow scientists and he shouldn't have to do anything beyond making it known. It was easy for Brougham to smear him and his work.

Throughout all of Young's scientific work, it is clear that he not only could make intuitive leaps such as his idea that light moves in waves, but he also had a practical streak which made him try to demonstrate even the most abstract thoughts in a way that would be audible or visible. When he experimented with sound, he blew smoke into long glass tubes so that he could see the effect of sound waves. With light, in one of the most inspired experiments in science, he thought of sending light through two narrow slits placed close together to make visible the effect of interference between overlapping waves. This has been called "Young's Experiment" and was used recently with electrons instead of light. To the bafflement of the experimenters, it was clear that electrons are individual particles which behave as if they are waves! This practical side of Young helps to explain the many down-to-earth contributions he made in engineering, vision, theory of the tides, and many others, as well as his invention of ingenious pieces of apparatus.

Why had only a few scientists thought to challenge Newton before or why hadn't Newton himself seen that a wave theory was required to explain some of his own observations? Newton had observed that when light passes through two plates of glass that have a thin layer of air or water between them, colored rings appear. They are even called Newton's Rings. But the great Newton was so convinced that if light traveled as waves it would be seen behind obstacles, that he couldn't see that the rings might be formed by the *interference* of light waves crossing each other. Scientists (and most of us) work within a set of rules that we have been taught. We call such a set of rules a paradigm. Anything new must fit within this limited way of explaining new observations because our minds cannot go beyond the limits of the paradigms we have learned. It is a rare person who can break out of this box and see how a new way of looking at the world with a different set of rules not only explains what we already know, but makes it possible to go beyond our old concepts. The need to introduce a new paradigm may explain why the most brilliant advances in physics and math come from young people who are not as set in their ideas as older people and, therefore, can question the accepted way of looking at familiar things.

Thanks largely to Lord Brougham's efforts, Young's theory and his discovery of interference dropped out of sight for the next 18 years. It was a twist of fortune that brought it back into the public eye. As we shall see, even then it was a Frenchman, Fresnel, who has ended up getting the lion's share of the credit in today's textbooks.

Young thought that the wave theory of light and his discovery of interference patterns were the most important contributions he had made or was ever likely to make. He was so discouraged when the scientific world ignored them that he played with the idea of deserting science. Fortunately, this was only a momentary reaction and it was quickly forgotten when he met Eliza Maxwell.

Eliza

Chapter 12

Shortly after he had delivered the last talk on light, he was surprised to have his servant announce that a young lady would like to see him. When she was ushered in, he was even more surprised to see that she was not a lady but was a young girl. She blushed slightly as she felt his gaze take in her face and figure. She was well aware how strange it must seem to him to have her call without an escort. But her voice was firm as she told him that she had some questions she'd like to ask him. Did he have a moment to talk to her now?

Young, who had forgotten his manners at this strange visit, quickly recovered and offered her a seat. She introduced herself as Eliza Maxwell, the daughter of James Maxwell, Esq., a man Young had met from time to time at social events. Thinking that the girl (for that is how he thought of her) may have picked him as someone who could introduce her to a young man who had caught her fancy, he asked how he could help her.

"I've been going to your lectures," she began, "and I'm afraid there are some parts of your wave theory that I don't understand."

"I suppose you are unhappy that my lectures are too difficult," he said defensively.

"Oh, no," she said firmly. "Your wave theory is elegant and your demonstration of interference is simply—well, beautiful. I'll admit that I've had to study the notes I've taken before the picture became clear."

Young was startled to learn that Eliza had taken notes at his lectures and had actually studied them. His surprise was even greater as he looked at her with new respect and again noted how very young she was. His thoughts must have shown in his face for she blurted out, "You think that only young men can be intelligent and eager to learn, don't you?"

This time he blushed for she seemed to guess his thoughts so well.

"I promise to take you seriously from now on. What did you want to ask?"

"I don't see how your wave theory as you've presented it can possibly explain the polarization of light. Don't you agree this is a problem?"

Young came back to the conversation with a start. He realized that he had been only half listening as he sat there admiring a shapely ankle that was visible below her ruffled skirt.

"You've touched on a sore point," he admitted. "In its present form I cannot explain how a light wave, which I am sure is similar to a sound wave, can become polarized in one plane. I may have to study the Iceland spar to see if it has special features in its construction that could explain it."

At this point, Eliza looked at her watch which dangled

gracefully from a neck chain and said, "Oh, dear, I mustn't stay any longer or Mama will be missing me. But I have one more question to ask." She took a deep breath and blurted out, "Papa is having a party next Friday in honor of my birthday. Since it is *my* birthday, I've been allowed to invite one guest. Would you honor us?"

The answer came to Young so readily and so warmly that he surprised himself. "The honor is mine. I'd be delighted."

With a twinkle in her eye she asked, "Would you please send a note to my father that you accept the invitation? He has no suspicion that I called on you in person. He's a fine man but a bit old fashioned."

Just as he was wondering which birthday it was, this frank and open woman said as she headed toward the door, "You'll find out how old I am at the party so I might as well tell you now. It will be my 16th birthday," and she swept out of the room leaving a dazed man to wonder why he was so anxious for Friday to come when this young lady was no older than his youngest sister.

As Young brushed his long hair before a mirror that evening, he saw that the man reflected in the mirror had an amused look. "Wait 'til I tell Hudson that I've met the most intriguing combination in my whole life of intelligence and beauty in one woman and she is only just about to be 16. I'm sure he'll think my hard work has affected my brain.

Thomas Young: Forgotten Genius

But she *is* very clever and I am sure Hudson will agree that she is most attractive."

On the evening of Eliza's birthday party, Young stepped out of a coach in front of the brightly-lit home of the Maxwells in Cavendish Square with torches set in every window and clusters of candles lighting up each room. To his relief, he could see that a few of the guests had already arrived although he knew he was early. As the butler took his hat, cape and walking stick, he spotted Eliza in the drawing room at the same moment that she saw him. She came toward him with the same warm smile that he remembered but which he thought he may have exaggerated in his memory of their first meeting. As she approached him in her elegant party dress, he realized that she *did* look mature for her age. He would have guessed her to be 18. She walked with poise and unselfconscious grace and her figure (if the arts of women's clothing was not deceiving him) was that of a grown woman.

"Do come in," she said. "I was afraid that you might have poked your head in front of a beam of light and become so engrossed in an experiment that you would forget my birthday party." Then taking his arm in hers, she said, "Mr. Young, I'd like you to meet my family."

The Maxwells were gathered in the drawing room and Young was introduced to Mr. and Mrs. Maxwell and their three other daughters. He and Eliza's father knew each other slightly. It was his first encounter with Mrs. Maxwell and she became his firm friend immediately when she told him how much she had admired his uncle, Dr. Brocklesby. Eliza introduced him to her sisters, "Maria, who is older than I am, and Emily and Caroline, who are still in school." It was obvious that the Maxwells were very fond of each other and the warmth of their greeting made him feel as if they included him in their circle.

"I must play the part of a good hostess," Eliza said with a slight shrug of her shoulders, "but I am sure you will find some lively conversations here and I'll be watching to see that you're not bored."

She led him to a group that was hotly arguing whether England should boycott American cotton that was grown with slave labor or whether this would cause too much unemployment in the cotton mills of England, and left him to his own devices.

Shortly before the announcement to enter the dining room, Young found Eliza at his side.

"Do you find time for anything besides your medical practice and your experiments?" she asked.

"Oh, yes," he assured her. "I've been to see Mrs. Siddons this past week. She's wonderful as Desdemona in Mr. Shakespeare's *Othello*. I also often go to the art galleries and I'm particularly fond of this new man, Turner, and his seascapes."

Thomas Young: Forgotten Genius

"Perhaps you would invite me to join you the next time you go to a gallery," she said as naturally as if young women were accustomed to ask men such questions. "You could tell me why you like Turner so much."

"I'm afraid I'm not an art expert," he protested. "I only know what I *don't* like. But there is something about Turner's clouds and skies that make me realize there is more to this universe than even our greatest minds can conceive."

At that moment the call to the table was announced and with a natural gesture that delighted him, Eliza offered her arm and made it clear that she wanted to sit with him. During the eight course meal, she drew out of him the story of how he had studied at Cambridge, had gone to Edinburgh on horseback and many of the amusing things that had happened to him in Gottingen. When he remembered particularly amusing encounters, she deftly brought in other nearby diners and drank in the pleasure that his stories gave to the other guests. Young began to wonder if this remarkable woman had been born mature!

The rest of the birthday party was a blur in Young's mind. Eliza would disappear among the guests from time to time, then reappear and resume their conversation as if it had never been interrupted. During the dances that followed, she wrote his name in her program more often than a hostess should have and he was grateful for all of the dancing lessons he had taken. He went home in a daze, unaware that for the first time in many weeks, his mind had not been on his experiments.

They saw each other often in the weeks following the party. At first he escorted her to museums, concerts and the theater with one or more of her sisters or her mother as chaperone. Then he began calling on her at home. The Maxwells tactfully withdrew after a time leaving them alone in the drawing room. Young felt confused about their relationship. He had no doubt that he was more strongly attracted to Eliza than he had ever been to any other woman. But he was 30 years old, nearly twice as old as she was. Could he really ask such a young person to marry him? In her typical straight-forward manner, Eliza answered the question for him. One day she caught him by each shoulder and kissed him full on the lips. They both knew that for them this meant they were engaged and would get married as soon as they had her parents' consent.

Young arranged a meeting with James Maxwell and in his typical, direct manner said, "Mr. Maxwell, I wish to have your permission to marry Eliza."

Mr. Maxwell was not surprised that this was what Young had in mind when he had asked to see him. He and his wife would have preferred that this attractive man might fall in love with Maria, their oldest daughter. It would have been a better match in terms of age and it was customary for older sisters to marry before their siblings, but it was so apparent that Young had eyes only for Eliza that the Maxwells, who liked Young very much, had decided they would give their consent if Maria agreed, which she did, enthusiastically.

There was one problem that bothered Mr. Maxwell and his wife, however. Thomas was the first man that Eliza had ever shown a special interest in. And she was only 16. Was this just an infatuation that would not last?

Responding to Young's request for his permission to marry his daughter, Mr. Maxwell said, "You know that the Missus and I think very highly of you and so do all of our children. But 16 is very young for a woman to swear vows that must last a lifetime. We are prepared to announce our daughter's engagement to you if you agree that the wedding will take place after her 17th birthday. Eliza is an impetuous young lady but you are a grown man and I suspect you may understand our concern about a hasty marriage."

"Eliza and I have already talked about this," Young answered, "and we have no objection to a year's engagement. We know our feeling for each other will not change in a year. I would use this year to build up my medical practice and I am in the middle of some new experiments on how the eye functions. Eliza and I agree this would not be the best time for us to get married. I thank you for accepting me into your family. I promise you'll never regret your decision."

Eliza

Eliza and Thomas were married on June 14, 1804 in a Church of England ceremony. Thomas Young, Sr. was sorry that this meant a complete break with the Society of Friends for his son but he admired the Maxwells and gave his reluctant approval to the marriage. He wasn't prepared. however, to see his oldest son married in an Anglican church and did not attend the ceremony. Thomas' mother represented his family and Hudson Gurney was his best man.

The Eyes Have It

Chapter 13

Young has been called the father of physiological optics.
He set about his work as if nobody before him had
investigated vision.

First, he carefully measured all the dimensions of the
eyeball (he used himself as the guinea pig in most of his
experiments). He fastened two small keys to the points of a
compass and pushed one key alongside his eye as far as he
could while it was turned to one side. Then he adjusted the
other key to be exactly over the pupil in the middle of his
eyeball. The distance between the compass points was the
diameter of his eyeball front to back and he also could
measure the curvature of his cornea with the same technique.
He mentions in his notes that this experiment was not
pleasant or easy and says that "with an eye less prominent,
this method might not have succeeded!" The length he found
was 23 mm and the radius of curvature was 7.87 mm.
Measurements made more than 100 years later gave 24 mm
and 7.70 mm.

Next he noticed that when he looked at a horizontal line
and held it the optimal distance from his eye to get a sharp
image, the line looked blurred when he turned it to be
vertical. He had discovered *astigmatism*. Today a chart is
used which has lines on it that are horizontal, vertical and
slanted. If a person has astigmatism, some of the lines look

Thomas Young: Forgotten Genius

darker than the others and eyeglasses can be made to correct for this problem. Young discovered this condition because he himself was slightly astigmatic but it didn't affect his vision enough for him to bother about it. He recognized immediately that glasses could be made to correct for astigmatism but 25 years passed before the first glasses were made to correct for this condition. Astigmatism can occur if either the cornea (the outer layer) of the eye or the lens is not perfectly curved.

He then discovered that light rays which fall on the eyes at a slant do not focus on the retina even though the eyes are perfectly normal. The same problem occurs with field glasses and telescopes. Rays of light which enter the eye near the center of the pupil—not at an angle—*do* focus on the retina but rays which enter at an angle do not. This is why our pupils are kept as small as possible and a camera has "stops" which make the opening smaller. This characteristic of lenses is called *spherical aberration* and good telescopes and field glasses have specially ground lenses to get around the problem. You can see for yourself that squinting makes objects look clearer by cutting off the light that is coming in to the eye at an angle. The Hubble telescope that was put into orbit is not working perfectly because it was not ground correctly to take care of spherical aberration.

Another problem that Young discovered is also due to

the nature of light itself. Blue colors are bent more than red when they pass through a lens. This can be seen with cheap field glasses when red and blue colors are seen around the edges of objects. This is called *chromatic aberration* and, like spherical aberration, it causes no major problems in vision but must be corrected for in artificial lenses, such as telescopes.

As we might have guessed, one of the problems he tackled was the question of how the eye adjusts to near and far vision. It was seven years since he had proposed that the lens changes its shape but he had had to withdraw his theory when the eminent Dr. Home said that he had a patient who could accommodate for near and far vision even with an eye from which one lens had been removed. This time Young devised a series of experiments that showed he was right.

First, he considered the problem. If a man looks at a candle that is about six feet from his eye and gets it into sharp focus, a similar candle that is further away looks blurred as long as the eye is focused on the first candle. If the eye now focuses on the far candle, it now looks sharp. How does the eye do this?

His brutal experiments on his own eyes showed that there is not enough room in the bony socket that the eye sits in to allow the eyeball to get longer. Earlier, he had shown this was true by substituting glass lenses for the eye. Now he had proof that the living eye cannot change its length as a

Thomas Young: Forgotten Genius

camera does.

Seven years earlier, his proof that the cornea does not change its curvature had not been very strong. He now thought of a brilliantly simple experiment to prove this point conclusively. Light is bent when it passes through the cornea and then through a watery fluid called the aqueous humor on its way to the retina. This bending occurs because the rays are going from air into a liquid—it is the phenomenon that is seen when an oar appears to be bent as it enters water. Young completely eliminated the bending effect (refraction) at the cornea by making a cup with a glass bottom, filling it with water and holding it against his eye. Now the light from an object was bent as it entered the cup but was not bent at the cornea because there was a similar fluid on both sides of the cornea. When his eye focused on a near object, he could see it clearly. When he then looked at a far object, it also became clear, showing that accommodation could occur and could not be due to the cornea.

With alternative theories out of the way, Young now had to answer the claim by Dr. Home that he had a patient who had no lens in one eye but could adapt perfectly with that eye. An eye specialist, Dr. Ware, generously permitted Young to examine patients who had had a lens removed. In no instance could they adapt to near and far vision with the bad eye. Now he was ready to tackle the problem of Dr. Home's patient. Dr. Home had mentioned the name of the patient, Benjamin Clark, when he gave his lecture in which he said Young was wrong, but he had said Mr. Clark had left England. Young discovered that Mr. Clark was now back. He located him and persuaded him to have his vision re-examined.

With a sense of drama that he may have learned from the theater, Young arranged that Dr. Home and he would re-examine Mr. Clark in Dr. Ware's office. Young had prepared for the examination carefully and Mr. Clark proved to be a cooperative subject. Dr. Ware seated Mr. Clark in a comfortable chair in a large room with many windows to let in as much light as possible. First he examined Clark's good eye, tying a cloth to cover the other eye. Standing near Mr. Clark, Young held up a card on which he had printed a large letter "R".

"What do you see?" Dr. Ware asked.

"The letter 'R'," Clark replied without hesitation.

"Is it clear or fuzzy?" Ware asked.

"Clear and sharp," came the answer.

Young then moved to the far end of the room and held up a card with "B" on it. Again Clark reported he could see the letter "B" clearly. The cloth was then placed over Mr. Clark's good eye and carefully tied so that he could see out only from the eye that had no lens.

When Young held up a card with the letter "P" at the far end of the room, Clark could only see a blur because he had no lens to help focus objects onto the retina. Dr. Ware then held a series of glass lenses in front of Clark's eye until he could see the "P" on the card clearly with sharp edges. When Young moved the card near to Mr. Clark, he could not read the letter at all even with the correcting lens in front of his eye—he was unable to adjust from near to far vision. They ran through the test again with the same result.

Young then turned to Dr. Home and asked, "Are you satisfied? Are there any other tests you would like to perform?"

"I am convinced," Dr. Home said. "Mr. Clark cannot adjust from far to near vision with his eye that has no lens."

Young waited for Dr. Home to offer an explanation of his previous wrong conclusion or at least an apology for having hurt Young's reputation for several years, but Home said nothing. Pulling on his gloves, he cleared his throat, said "Good day, gentlemen," and walked out of the room.

Dr. Home would have been a good target for a libel suit or a duel of honor but Young was so much of a gentleman that he didn't even record his reaction in his note book.

Chapter l4

About the time Young was born, a paper was read at the Royal Society describing a shoemaker named Harris who couldn't tell a red stocking from a gray one. He said he couldn't pick berries because he could not tell which ones were ripe. This condition of color blindness attracted wide public attention when, just at the time Young was starting his medical studies, the famous chemist, John Dalton, described his own problems with color. To Dalton, blood looked green and a leaf looked the same color as red sealing wax.

Young began his studies of color vision in his own typical manner. He wanted to see for himself and to use quantitative measurements. He passed sunlight through a slit in a curtain, then through a prism and had it fall on a large wall. Under the best conditions, he could make out 150 to 200 different shades of color. As he turned his head, he could still see the colors until he was looking out of the corners of his eyes. Since he regarded light as waves or vibrations, he wrote, "Now, as it is almost impossible to conceive each sensitive point of the retina to contain an infinite number of particles, each capable of vibrating in perfect unison with every possible undulation, it becomes necessary to suppose the number [of cones, we would say] limited, for instance to the principal colors, red, yellow and blue...." [9] He not only experimented by mixing different colors but he made a spinning top which revolved so fast that the colors on it blended to give all the colors of the rainbow, depending on which colors he painted onto the top and how strong each color was. He made a color diagram which had a triangle with red, green and violet at the corners and the colors made by mixing any of the two along each side. This diagram is in many textbooks although they usually show red, yellow and blue at the corners. The reason Young chose red, green and violet instead of the primary colors is because light when mixed does not give the same colors as paint when mixed. The difference is not important as far as understanding his theory of color vision is concerned. His chart is a better representation of how we see colors because it will give white when all of the colors of light are mixed but a mixture of pure paints will not do this.

When Young published his theory of color vision, no one knew about the nerves in the retina. We now know that they have three kinds of receptors. He had made a purely imaginative leap that has since been supported by modern neurophysiological research. His theory was not popularized until nearly 50 years later when a German physicist, Helmholtz, rediscovered it while reading the transactions of the Royal Society. Helmholtz was lost in admiration of Young and gave him full credit for the theory and modified it only slightly. Today it is taught to medical students as the Young-Helmholtz Theory of color vision. As was pointed out to me by Professor John Z. Young of Oxford (a descendant of Thomas Young), this was the first suggestion of the valuable idea which is now the basis underlying all studies of the nervous system that the brain does not merely receive information, but also integrates information which arrives by many parallel channels, greatly expanding the power of our senses.

Chapter 15

Benjamin Thompson (later Count Rumford), a native of New England who had fought with the British in the American War of Independence, wanted the new scientific knowledge being discovered to be used for the benefit of mankind. Largely through his efforts, the Royal Institution was founded and one of its first actions was to appoint two men to explain science to lay people. Sir Humphrey Davy, already a well-known chemist and Thomas Young were appointed Professors for two year terms to give a series of lectures which became fashionable for educated men and women to attend. Davy's lectures were very popular but Young failed to talk at a level that non-scientists could understand and by the end of his second series, the audience had dwindled considerably. Hudson Gurney wrote in his *Memoir of Thomas Young*, "Dr. Young, whose profound knowledge of the subjects he taught no one will venture to question, lectured in the same theater and to an audience similarly constituted to that which was attracted to Davy, but he found the number of his attendants diminish daily and for no other reason than that he adopted too severe and didactic a style. He was apt to pass the capacities of his audience who at this time were led to attend more as a matter of fashion, than from a love of research and who for the most part had little previous knowledge." Although the details are not available, there is some indication that when Young's appointment was not renewed, the parting was not amicable. His lectures and demonstrations may not have pleased his audience which had little or no knowledge of science, but they constitute one of the most impressive reviews of science ever assembled and contained new ideas in many areas that were far ahead of his time.

For several years after their marriage, Eliza may have wondered if Young had married her because he needed a secretary but she seems to have enjoyed working with him enormously. Together they put the two-year lecture course he had given at the Royal Institute into shape for publishing. When they had finished after three years of hard work, the publication added up to two volumes, each about 750 pages long. The first volume and part of the second covered the entire field of physics except for the part of astronomy that he felt required mathematics too difficult for most readers to follow. The second volume listed 20,000 papers. theses and publications that he had used to prepare the lectures. It is mind-boggling to think of collecting 20,000 references before there were computers, Xerox machines or even typewriters.

He believed that demonstrations were necessary in order for an audience to understand science. He certainly was right as far as his own lectures were concerned. His mind leaped so quickly and penetrated so deeply that even experts had trouble understanding him. Many of the fashionable women who never had been taught science, came to his lectures and may have just sat there thinking about their new hats as they quickly got lost in the labyrinth of his explanations. He put on more than 40 demonstrations including several for which he invented the equipment and personally drew the illustrations for the book. He tossed off these inventions as easily as Mozart produced music, but despite a large number of elegant illustrations, he lost those in the audience who were not able to follow his rapid thoughts.

Two of his inventions became the basis for important instruments that remain in use (with modern improvements) to the present day.

One of these, shown in Figure 4, is the forerunner of the recording barometer which measures the "heaviness of air" and is used to forecast weather changes. A weight (C) is attached to a string (I). The string passes over a pulley and is carefully wrapped around a vertical pole (AB) the way a thread is wrapped on a spool. The coiled thread holds up a cylinder (H). When the weight is released, the cylinder drops as the string unwinds so that a writing point which touches the cylinder traces a spiral as the cylinder goes around. Two very light balls, (D and E) fly out as the axis is turned and two weights (F and G) which sit on a ledge, also move out from the axis. When the balls and the weights are thrown out just enough to balance the friction of the air (plus the weight of the balls), the rate of spinning can be read off the cylinder which has evenly spaced vertical time lines drawn on it. Today mercury and springs are used instead of weights and we say the barometric pressure is rising or falling, promising good weather or storms.

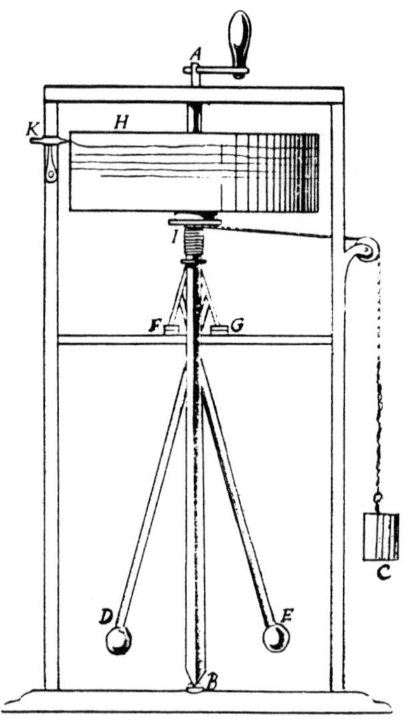

Figure 4

Barometer and Kymograph

Modified from Wood, A. 1954

A Versatile Man

It was modified by Karl Ludwig, one of the world's most famous physiologists (who gave Young full credit for the original invention) to measure blood pressure, muscle contractions and the movements of the intestines and many other physiological activities. This modified instrument, called the kymograph, was used for the next 100 years by great physiologists such as Pavlov and Sherrington and was still being used by medical students and researchers as late as the 1960's. (It has since been replaced by electronic recorders).

Perhaps the fashionable ladies, even though they had not been taught science, could understand his very simple, clever device to illustrate wave motions which he called a Ripple Tank. A wire dips into a trough of water and is made to vibrate. The trough has a glass bottom with a light below and a mirror above which allows the audience to see the waves and how they interfere with each other. For many years, every English lecturer in physics used this apparatus.

A quick look at the subjects Young covered shows that he lectured on:

Drawing, writing and measurements
The physical properties of liquids and gases
Reservoirs, canals, piers and harbors
Theory of sailing boats
Water and air pumps
Acoustics

Thomas Young: Forgotten Genius

Optics

Astronomy, gravitation, tides

Cohesion of molecules (capillary attraction)

Heat and electricity

Climate and winds

Vegetation and animal life

A mere listing of the subjects does not show why in 1934, 127 years after their publication, the lectures were described as the "greatest and most original of all lecture courses" and the reviewer wrote that "no such authoritative catalogue, even of the most select classical works of modern science [from one person] is likely to appear again." [10] From a closer look at a few of his key lectures we can learn how his mind worked, putting together observations that were not obviously connected. He said:

"The phenomena of nature resemble the scattered leaves of Sibylline prophecies; a word only, or a single syllable, is written on each leaf, which, when separately considered, conveys no instruction to the mind; but when, by the labour of patient investigation, every fragment is replaced in its appropriate connection, the whole begins at once to speak a harmonious language." [11]

As an example of how Young brought different ideas together, we know that he took the motions of water, sound and light and brought them together as wave motions which changed our ideas of tides, acoustics and light. With remarkable insight, he understood the importance of what we now call the kinetic energy of a moving body and was the first person to use the word *energy* to describe it. He calculated that a small grain of sand could go through a solid wall if it were moving fast enough. Pilots of airplanes who have had a small bird hit a vital part of their plane (and lived to tell about it) know how correct he was!

His approach to science was not merely to solve isolated problems, but, using fairly few rules, he made new connections which would apply to our daily lives. Movies, sound reproduction, television and even landing on the moon were made possible by his basic studies. When Young realized that metals were being used more and more in bridges and buildings he measured the resistance of both wooden beams and such metals to compression and bending. Modern textbooks of physics call this Young's Modulus of Elasticity. It is the ratio of applied stress to the resulting strain and it is still taught to architects and engineers. He extended this idea to liquids and studied capillary attraction. He even calculated the distance over which molecular forces can attract and repel each other and had the audacity to calculate the first estimate ever made of the diameter of a molecule. He was wrong by a factor of 100 but considering the apparatus he had to work with and the state of knowledge at that time, even to attempt such a measurement was amazing.

Thomas Young: Forgotten Genius

At the time he gave his lectures, many scientists, especially the French, thought that heat was a very thin fluid that they called caloric. Other scientists said heat was caused by the motion of particles. It had just been shown that a thermometer gets warm even when it is placed beyond the red end of the spectrum that is thrown on a wall by a prism. This showed that light waves beyond the visible spectrum can produce heat. Young in his clear-thinking way said, "if heat is not a substance that exists by itself, it must be a quality that changes within a substance and this quality can only be motion." He then linked up the idea of heat vibrations with his observations on light and sound and for the first time proposed that beyond visible light, the spectrum at each end contains vibrations that we can't see and beyond audible sounds there are vibrations we cannot hear. He was as usual far ahead of his time. He even showed that crystals of silver nitrate darken when exposed to light beyond the violet end of the spectrum. This might be called the first (crude) photograph ever reported!

Young's lecture on balance and motion give a good picture of how he thought of complex and abstract ideas in down-to-earth terms and could devise relatively simple experiments to test his theories. In his lectures he said:

"In the equilibrium of animals we may observe many examples illustrative of the properties of the centre of gravity. When a person stands on one foot and leans forward, in the attitude which is usually exhibited in the statues of Mercury, the other foot is elevated behind, in order to bring back the centre of gravity so as to be vertically over some part of the foot on which he stands. But...the basis it affords is really very narrow; hence, when we attempt to stand on one foot, we find it often necessary to use a muscular exertion in order to bring the point of support to that side toward which we are beginning to fall; and when the basis is still more contracted, the body never remains at rest, but by a succession of actions of this kind, sometimes too minute to be visible, it is kept in a state of perpetual vibration...hence, by habit, the arts of rope-dancers and balancers are acquired." [12]

After making these observations on himself, he actually learned how to walk on a tight-rope and verified for himself that we maintain our balance by the continual contractions of many small muscles which produce a smooth total contraction of a large muscle. Modern studies show that he was correct and today many neurological conditions are recognized by the small tremors that are characteristically produced.

Not only a brilliant experimenter and scientist, Young anticipated the thoughts of modern physicists and philosophers long before Einstein's Theory of Relativity and the birth of quantum mechanics completely altered the conventional view of the world we live in.

Thomas Young: Forgotten Genius

In 1807 he wrote: "Even the ultimate particles of matter may be permeable to the causes of attractions of various kinds, especially if these causes are immaterial; nor is there anything in the unprejudiced study of physical philosophy that can induce us to doubt the existence of immaterial substances; on the contrary, we see analogies that lead us almost directly to such an opinion. There are semimaterial existences which produce the phaenomena of electricity and magnetism. Higher still, perhaps, are the causes of gravitation....The more refined and immaterial appear to pervade freely the grosser. It seems, therefore, natural to believe that the analogy may be continued still further until it [gives] rise into existence [substances that are] absolutely immaterial and spiritual. We know not but that thousands of spiritual worlds may exist unseen forever by human eyes. [We] may speculate with freedom on the possibility of independent worlds; some existing in different parts of space, others pervading each other, unseen and unknown, in the same space, and others again to which space may not be a necessary mode of existence." [13]

Compare this speculation with some modern views on the ultimate reality of our world. Every thing that we know about the world around us has come through electrical impulses which are sent from sense receptors such as sight, touch, etc. to our brains. Until modern times, we were sure that a real world exists with hard objects like chairs and baseball bats. Then physicists performed a simple experiment devised originally by Thomas Young to prove that light moves in waves. The experiment consisted of a screen with two slits in it which was set between a source and a detector. In the new experiment, electrons were used instead of light. Electrons were shown to leave a source as individual particles and were detected after passing through the slits as individual particles. However, the pattern on the detector showed that they had traveled as waves. The possibility has to be considered that things "out there" are waves and appear to be solid objects only because our nervous system receives signals that say "particles" (after a wave has collapsed into a particle when it meets a sense receptor). We think we live in a world of solid objects because an unsolid wave has become a solid particle. Brilliant physicists and philosophers have tried to answer what is really happening "out there" when waves "collapse" into particles. A recent suggestion is that the real world may consist of holograms which are the patterns formed when waves interfere with each other (a phenomenon discovered by Young). Another idea called the Many Worlds Interpretation of Quantum Mechanics suggests that there are many worlds co-existing with ours, all of which consist of non-material waves. Young's speculation made nearly 200 years earlier is uncanny!

A French physicist and astronomer, Dr. Arago, who

became a friend of Young's, studied his lectures and said that he found it was hard to believe that this was the work of only one man. He said it was more like the output of the entire Royal Society!

But more was yet to come.

Appointment to St. George's Hospital

Chapter 16

In December, 1809, Young passed an examination and was elected a Fellow of the Royal College of Physicians. This was an honor given only to outstanding physicians. However, in spite of this success as a doctor, Young continued to be upset that his practice did not flourish and Eliza became depressed to see him bothered so greatly.

The following year, St. George's Hospital in London had a vacancy on its staff. This hospital was, at that time, one of the most important hospitals in all of England with a long list of impressive sponsors. An appointment to St. George's meant that a physician had reached the top of his profession.

"I had an impulse to submit my name for the vacancy," he told Eliza one day, "but the appointment is very political and there are already two highly qualified applicants. Dr. Cabbell has a great deal of support in London and a large family with several influential members to support him. The other strong candidate is Dr. Roget who is the nephew of the very powerful politician, Sir Romilly. Everyone expects that his uncle will soon be appointed Lord Chancellor, the highest judge in England. This will obtain many votes for Dr. Roget. I don't have a chance against such competition."

To his surprise, Eliza turned on him fiercely. "What do you mean you don't have a chance?" she challenged. "You have many influential friends who would favor you and

Thomas Young: Forgotten Genius

Hudson would support you to the hilt. I think it's about time a hospital as important as St. George's should have someone on its staff who is up-to-date on the advances that are occurring in the sciences. You yourself have told me that the new sciences are going to change the whole world of medical treatment. I've never seen you turn away from any problem just because it is difficult. Throw yourself into the fight for this appointment and make your wife happy to see you on the staff of St. George's Hospital!"

Without a word, Young sat down and began to write letters to everyone he knew who was a voting member of the Hospital. (Today, doctors are appointed to the staffs of hospitals by members of the medical community. In Young's day, each hospital had a large number of important people who were in politics, law, the clergy, universities and other occupations. They contributed financially to the hospital and had a vote whenever a replacement was required.)

Because Young entered his name late, he received several apologetic letters stating that votes had already been pledged to his competitors. However, once Young entered the contest, he and Gurney wrote letters and called on individuals night and day. The election was held on January 24, 1811 and proved to be the closest election the hospital had ever had. The voting was: Dr. Young, 100 votes; Dr. Cabbell, 92 votes; Dr. Roget, 51 votes; others, 4 votes.

When Eliza heard the good news, she told the friend

who informed her, that she felt Thomas would never again fret about his career as a physician. A feeling of depression which had been bothering her lifted and never returned.

Thomas Young: Forgotten Genius

Hudson Gurney

Photograph courtesy of David Gurney

Hudson Marries Mag—at Last

Chapter 17

It was no surprise to Thomas or Eliza when Hudson told them that he was engaged to his long-time friend, Margaret, and that their marriage would take place early the next year. For more than 20 years, Hudson had been enchanted by this woman he had first met as "the rattish Mag" when she had come from Scotland to stay at Earlham, his uncle John's home.

Hudson had begun to visit this wild household full of teen age children when he was 15 years old and was living at Youngsbury. Thomas had listened fascinated as Hudson described his visits. His uncle was a banker and a very liberal Quaker who left the raising of their three daughters and one son to his wife, Catherine. Besides his four cousins, Hudson's brother Richard and his sisters Anna and Agatha were also often there—and then there was Mag.

Aunt Catherine felt that children of good stock should have as much freedom as possible and they would turn out to be fine citizens. Today, we would not think the behavior of these children was anything unusual, but for those days when strict upbringing was the rule, especially among Quakers, Hudson found himself thrown into teasing and fighting situations or was excluded from the group in ways that only teenagers can invent to make each other unhappy. They were all bright children and pulled books out of the well-stocked Gurney library to read choice passages to each other while seated in the branches of trees or wherever they stopped to catch their breath after some wild game of tag.

Mag who was 13 when Hudson first met her, had quickly established herself as someone dangerous to play tricks on. Perhaps she found it necessary to assert herself not to be overwhelmed by all the cousins, but an insult thrown her way was likely to end up in a brawl with violent hair-pulling and the marks of Mag's finger nails on her opponent's arms and legs. Even though Mag threw on whatever clothes happened to be available and made no attempt to comb her hair or try to be attractive, Hudson was fascinated by this fiery, independent young woman and tried to get her to like him. She laughed at his efforts and declared that she could never admire anyone who questioned a word of the Bible. She knew that cynicism about the Bible was one of Hudson's prized teen age sources of argument. He never dared to tell her how he could hardly wait for his next visit to Earlham to see her pert nose and hear her saucy words flung out at him through a cloud of unbrushed long, raven hair.

When the cousins emerged from their teens, just as their mother had believed, they became solid but lively citizens and one by one married, started families and plunged into community affairs. Mag, too, came out of adolescence and shed her "rattish" habits as if they were a temporary skin she no longer needed. She began to dress with care, move with grace and poise and Hudson was entirely under the spell of this new gracious and charming woman who still had an air of independence that set her off from all the other women he had met.

When Mag had her 20th birthday, Hudson asked her if she would marry him.

"Surely you know," she answered, "that I haven't had eyes for any other man since your first visit to Earlham. You were so handsome and full of fun and yet there was a shyness about you that went straight to my heart."

"You've certainly kept your feelings secret all these years," Hudson protested.

"If those cousins and sisters of yours had known that I liked you, their teasing would have driven me mad," Mag laughed. "But that's all in the past now."

"Then your answer is yes," Hudson said, scarcely able to believe that his wishes were finally coming true.

"I am afraid I cannot say that right now," she said. I cannot marry at this time because my mother in Scotland is too old to move and she may need my care at any time. But that is not the only reason. I hope you will understand exactly what I am about to say. I shall never marry anyone else as long as you are still single, but before I can take the serious step of becoming your wife, I must try living independently and find out who I am and what talents I have.

If I marry now, I'll spend the rest of my life wondering about the parts of me that never had a chance to develop."

"How long do you think this would take?" he asked.

"I have no idea, Hudson," she replied. "You are a wonderful target for every single young woman who meets you. I should not blame you if you could not wait for foolish me to settle down but whether it's two years or ten, I know that this is something I must do."

In the years that followed, Hudson and Mag saw each other from time to time but the subject of marriage was carefully avoided. Hudson, after leaving Youngsbury, joined his father in the banking business and for a few years was content to write poetry and translate Greek and Latin classics into English. He never forgot his reforming instincts that had led him to go to Paris during the French Revolution and he decided to make his mark by standing for a seat in Parliament. Eventually, he served six successive terms, becoming known particularly for his firm anti-slavery position and his support of scholarship.

Mag meanwhile tried her hand at painting, writing and music and found that she did not have the talent to make a name for herself in any of these fields. She then tried nursing but soon found that the horrors of the sick wards were more than she could stand when so little could be done for those in pain. Finally, she discovered that she had a talent for teaching. The girls responded to her mixture of impatience with the rules of society which limited the horizons of women and her deeply held belief in honesty, goodness and morality. It must have been easy for many a teenager to get a "crush" on such an attractive teacher. With the passage of time, the number of Mag's single friends got smaller and smaller. Her social life began to narrow and she found herself thinking more and more often of life as the wife of Hudson Gurney.

When Mag learned that her mother, whom she had not seen for many years, had died peacefully in her sleep, her reaction was partly regret that she had not been close to her mother since she had been a child and partly the admission to herself that she was now ready for marriage.

After waiting several months after the death of Mag's mother, Eliza and Thomas invited her to their home for dinner along with Hudson. As Mag thought about the upcoming evening, she wondered whether Hudson would still want to marry her or had he settled so comfortably into the life of a wealthy bachelor that he would not want to change? She looked over her tweed skirts and plain blouses that she wore as a teacher and decided that even though she was now a mature woman of 33, she could still wear a silk skirt that swirled as she turned and an off-the-shoulder blouse of the same material that the younger women were wearing that year. Adding a cape that clasped under her chin she hoped her outfit would please a conservative older bachelor and at the same time that he would find her attractive.

Hudson had never gotten over his earlier fascination with Mag and as he saw how she had become a confident, mature woman, he decided to dare ask her once again if she might consider marriage. In addition to the strong attraction she had exerted on him for many years, he longed for someone to look after his needs and be a help mate in his busy political life. This time the answer was "yes". They quickly agreed to a wedding in Norwich at his family's home but they decided to have a reception in the house at St. James Place in London that Hudson had just purchased for his wife-to-be which she would furnish before the wedding.

The night of the reception, Thomas and Eliza were in their coach, riding through the brightly lit streets of London to the party.

"Isn't it amazing that our streets at night are as bright as daylight," she exclaimed. "I am so glad the city council accepted your recommendation that gas lighting is perfectly safe. It has been only a few years since our wedding when the coachmen had to carry torches to find their way in the dark."

"I will never forget the night of your 16th birthday, Eliza," Thomas mused, "when my coach turned the corner and I saw your parents' house blazing out of the darkness with torches in every window."

Hudson Marries Mag—at Last

The house at St. James Place was well lit and the reception was large, noisy and a great success with the very best food, drinks and music that an affluent banker could provide. Everyone exclaimed at the faultless taste Mag had shown in furnishing the large house and the happy couple held hands and looked like school children. Thomas, as usual, threw himself into the party. He danced every dance, sang with other guests at the piano and drank more than was usual for him. On the ride back, Eliza took Thomas' hand in hers and said, "I love to see the party side of you emerge as it did tonight. You spend so much of your time being a serious hard-working scientist that I am delighted to see that the light side of you is still there. I remember that I had some of this same feeling at my 16th birthday party. I had been wondering if such a bright, dedicated scientist and scholar would be attracted to a young thing like me, but when I saw how you responded to the dancing and gay spirit of the party, I knew that I had a chance." She squeezed his hand and said, "How lucky I am to have not only a genius as a husband but a wonderful man, too!" Thomas squeezed her hand in return and said, "You make me wish I *hadn't* convinced the city council to make our streets so bright but, after all, we are a sober couple, married eight years already," and he drew the side curtains closed.

Thomas Young: Forgotten Genius

Margaret Barclay (Hudson Gurney's wife)

Courtesy of David Gurney

A New Puzzle

Chapter 18

A great many of the Nobel Prizes in physics have been awarded to scientists for ideas they had before they were 30 years old. It seems to take a young mind to break through old barriers (paradigms) and see new possible answers to old problems in physics. After their brilliant breakthroughs, physicists continue to do very useful work but they rarely, if ever, come forth with the remarkable new insights that they had earlier. Young seemed to know this himself. He told Eliza and his friends that he was not going to do any more research in physics but would concentrate on medical problems. But even he did not know himself that well. He had such a versatile mind, well-prepared in so many aspects of human knowledge, that he was able to tackle a puzzle in a brand new field and once again produce a phenomenal achievement: he deciphered hieroglyphic Egyptian writing.

In the month of May, 1814, Eliza was drawing up a list of the things they would take with them for their annual stay at Worthing-by-the-sea.

"I'm leaving books and scientific equipment to you," she said. "After ten years with you I still never know what will catch your attention next. Worthing is no longer the fashionable resort it once was," she went on. "There won't be as many educated people there and I'm afraid we'll have many evenings with no plans."

Thomas Young: Forgotten Genius

"I won't get bored," he responded cheerfully. "In fact, I'm looking forward to some free time. There's always some problem waiting to be solved. I am planning to have a go at the Rosetta Stone. I'll put a rubbing of the Stone in the pile of books and articles I'm taking along."

What is the Rosetta Stone, a copy of which Young had almost casually taken on his summer vacation as an amusing puzzle for him to work on during rainy days at the seashore? Why was this tablet, found by Napoleon Bonaparte's soldiers in Egypt, so important?

Napoleon Bonaparte had enlisted in the French army in 1776. His military ability quickly moved him up the ranks and when the French, who were at war with England, needed a military leader, they turned to him. He advised against an invasion of England across the English Channel because the British navy was too strong. Instead, he recommended that the French conquer Egypt which was ruled by a weak Turkish government and was a vital stop on the route from England to its rich trading colony, India. Napoleon's army had no difficulty defeating the Turks and gaining control of the ancient land of Egypt.

But Napoleon was more than just a military man. Under his personal orders, France set up a system of laws called the Code Napoleon, founded the Bank of France and reorganized the educational system. He showed the breadth of his interests when he had a large group of French scholars and scientists accompany his army into Egypt. Their reports of this ancient civilization with its enormous pyramids, sphinxes, obelisks and temples of huge stones excited the imagination of thousands in Europe.

The British reacted to his attempt to cut off their trade with India by sending Admiral Nelson to sink the French navy. He finally cornered the French ships in a bay off the coast of Egypt and destroyed it in what is called the Battle of the Nile. Napoleon's army was cut off from its supplies and he had to flee to France in a small boat that slipped through the British blockade.

The British took over and the country became a happy hunting ground for scholars and fortune hunters who dismembered and carried off many ancient treasures. Adventurous travelers brought back papyri and carved stones which became the topics of conversation at fashionable dinners and parties. Many of the huge structures in Egypt were covered with hieroglyphs—a strange kind of picture writing featuring birds, people, household objects and unrecognizable symbols. No living Egyptians were able to read the old writing. Scholars in many countries threw themselves into attempts to translate this mysterious language and satisfy their hunger to learn more about the ancient civilization. Even some of the rulers of European countries became amateur archaeologists and linguists.

In August, 1799, one of Napoleon's soldiers had come

Thomas Young: Forgotten Genius

across a stone near a town which the French called Rosetta, about 35 miles from Alexandria in Egypt. Chiseled into its surface was an inscription in three parts. The first was in the sacred picture writing of the Egyptian priests, which we now call hieroglyphic signs. The second passage. also in Egyptian looked like stenographer's shorthand and came to be called demotic and the third was in Greek. The French recognized how valuable the Stone was and sent copies of the inscriptions to many European scholars. Two years later, when Napoleon's army had to leave Egypt, the British seized the Rosetta Stone and placed it in the British Museum where it is prominently displayed today.

The stone, which was originally about 5 feet by 2 ½ feet, had lost almost 2 feet from the top which had contained a portion of the hieroglyphic writing and a small piece from the bottom but most of the Greek text could be translated. It stated that an assembly of the Friends of the Gods had held a meeting in Memphis on March 27, l96 B.C. (as we calculate it) to honor King Ptolemy V. They had ordered that the honors they had bestowed on Ptolemy were to be carved in hard stone (basalt) in the "writing of the speech of the Gods" (hieroglyphic), the "writing of the Gods" (demotic) and in Greek. These tablets were to be distributed throughout Egypt and displayed in all of the important temples. Since the two Egyptian texts carried the same message as the Greek portion, it looked as if it would be a simple matter to match the Greek against the Egyptian texts and then the thousands of inscriptions on temple walls, obelisks and papyri would be readable. But the task proved to be impossibly difficult until Thomas Young decided it was a puzzle he wanted to solve.

Young, besides everything else he was doing, had accepted the position as Foreign Corresponding Secretary of the Royal Society shortly after graduating from Cambridge. He kept this position for the rest of his life because it introduced him to almost all of the scholars of Europe and, as the Foreign Secretary, he could exchange his latest papers with theirs. When Young sat down to decipher the puzzle of the demotic writing, he knew that only two other people had believable claims that they had made any progress on the problem. He had corresponded with a man named de Sacy, a leading figure in ancient history who worked in Paris. Although Young did not meet de Sacy personally until several years later, they struck up a warm friendship. De Sacy had identified Ptolemy, Alexandria and Alexander from the demotic writing on the Rosetta Stone but he wasn't able to go on from there.

The other man who claimed to have made some progress with the demotic script was a Swedish diplomat named Akerblad who was an expert in Coptic, a language related to old Egyptian that was still in common use in Egypt until about 1600 A.D. Akerblad claimed he had identified 16 names and words from their similarity to Coptic but since he was unable to establish an alphabet or use his results to decipher the rest of the inscription, he couldn't make any further progress.

In their correspondence, de Sacy mentioned that a brilliant young man named Champollion was also working on the Rosetta Stone but so far had not gotten anywhere. Like Young, Champollion had shown his genius at an early age. Born in 1790, (17 years after Young), he fell in love with ancient Egypt when he was only ten and declared that he would dedicate his life to the study of that old civilization. This confident young man, hardly more than a boy, vowed that he would translate the writing on the Rosetta Stone. With his eyes firmly fixed on his goal, by the time he was 17, he had learned the Middle Eastern languages of Hebrew, Syriac, Chaldee and Coptic as well as Greek and Latin. His older brother, an archaeologist, introduced him to de Sacy. De Sacy encouraged him in his interest in Egypt but advised him to steer away from the Rosetta Stone because it "would not produce any result". About three years later, Champollion obtained a position at the University in the town of Grenoble where his brother was on the faculty. He was more determined than ever that he would succeed and he sketched out an ambitious plan for a large work on the people, the buildings, the geography and many other aspects of Egypt which would stake out his claim as the premier scholar of Egyptology. He called the entire projected series "L'Egypte sous les Pharaons" (Egypt under the Pharaohs). Volume I, an introduction, soon appeared. A second volume was published in 1814. Champollion, with sublime arrogance, promised that he would produce a complete translation of the Rosetta Stone in the near future. In the preface, he wrote that the books contained new translations of demotic and hieroglyphic words. An alert reviewer might have noticed that the demotic words had already been published by de Sacy and Akerblad and there were no translated hieroglyphic words.

Eliza had followed Young's scientific work with interest and understanding. She had astonished him at their very first meeting by her questions about his wave theory of light. This wasn't just a trick to get him interested in her. She worked side by side with him in editing the huge volumes of his lectures. However, when it came to foreign languages, she had to admit that she was a novice.

"Do you plan to use the words de Sacy and Akerblad have translated?" she asked her husband.

"I have a great deal of respect for de Sacy," he replied, "and I will keep in mind the three names he deciphered. However, I have strong doubts about Akerblad's work and I will try to put the letters he says he has translated out of my mind. In my experience, it is much harder to solve a problem if you start off with ideas that may be incorrect and

Thomas Young: Forgotten Genius

I want to attack this puzzle with a fresh approach. If
Akerblad is correct, he should have been able to develop an
alphabet from the names he has published but it is several
years since he made the claim and there's been no word
from him since."

"No one has translated any of the hieroglyphic language.
Akerblad and de Sacy only mention the demotic writing,"
Eliza commented. "If I know you, you're going to leap frog
the demotic writing and try to match the Greek with the
hieroglyphs. Am I right?"

"Not this time, Liza" he replied. "There are only a few
lines of hieroglyphs left at the top of the Stone. We don't
know how much is missing. I'm making a guess that the path
to reading the hieroglyphic signs lies through deciphering the
demotic first. The demotic signs remind me of Arabic and
Persian which I've loved since I was a young boy and I'm
eager to match the Greek portion of the Stone with the
writing of the scribes. The hieroglyphs, I'd bet, will prove
to be related to the demotic." Once again his intuition was
correct.

In his typical orderly fashion, Young carefully copied out
the demotic text from his rubbing of the Rosetta Stone using
all the skill he had acquired in his youth to make his
drawings as exact as if he had Xeroxed the inscription. He
then cut the paper into lines and pasted them onto sheets of
paper with spaces between each line. In the spaces he wrote

the Greek portion of the Stone. He didn't expect they would match since the Egyptian writing may not even have been alphabetical but may have represented ideas or symbols, like Chinese. However, by looking for words that appeared more than once in Greek and finding demotic signs that also appeared the same number of times, he gradually built up an alphabet that enabled him to guess new words. In one of the most incredible mental feats ever recorded, by the end of the summer he had a virtually complete translation of the demotic text. And he had only worked on it during his spare time when he was not seeing patients!

The text with Young's translation was published in a scientific journal, Archaeologia, the following year and was reprinted the same year in the Museum Criticum of Cambridge. Not another Egyptian word from the Rosetta Stone was deciphered and published by anyone but Young for the next seven years. Although Young was invariably modest in his writing and speech, his enormous confidence in his ability to solve any problem that he set his mind to, comes through clearly in a letter he sent to Hudson Gurney during his summer at Worthing:

"You tell me that I shall astonish the world if I make out this inscription. I think it on the contrary astonishing that it should not have been made out already, and that I should find the task so difficult as it appears to me. Certainly the labour of a few days would be sufficient for the comparison of an equal number of lines in any ordinary unknown language, aided by a literal translation {the Greek portion}, so as to identify pretty satisfactorily all the words that occurred more than once, and to ascertain their meaning; but I have been a month [!] upon this, and have still several passages that occur more than once which I cannot completely identify, or at least understand. But by far the greater part of the words I have ascertained with tolerable certainty...." [14]

Although new scholarly findings were often published in journals as we do today, a great deal of information was circulated as correspondence because of the slowness of the publication process. Priorities and a keen desire to know the latest developments were important even then! Young fired off his translation to de Sacy in the Fall of 1814 and asked for the latest information on Akerblad's and Champollion's progress. De Sacy replied immediately:

"I have very strong reservations concerning the validity of M. Akerblad's alphabet. M. Champollion also claims to have read the demotic script. I have more confidence in Akerblad's work than in Champollion's but until they publish their work, I think it is only fair to suspend judgment." [15]

In the following year de Sacy explained even more clearly why he believed that Young was far ahead of his competitors in a letter which was published in the Museum *Criticum* with Young's demotic translation—but without the following remarkable passage which Young left out to spare embarrassment to de Sacy:

"Monsieur, I have received your translation [of the Rosetta Stone] that I do not have in front of me at this moment, it being lent to M. Champollion's brother at his request after he received a letter from you....I think, Monsieur, that you are further ahead today and that you can read a large part of the Egyption {demotic} text. If I have any advice to give you, it is not to communicate your discoveries to M. Champollion. It is possible that he might claim priority. He seeks to make people believe that he has discovered many words of the Rosetta inscription. I am afraid this is only charlatanism; I even add that I have strong reasons to think this....In addition, I can not be persuaded that if Akerblad or Champollion have made progress, they would not have made their discoveries public. This would be a rare modesty and neither of them appear to me to be capable of this." [16]

Although correspondence between the English and French went on during the Napoleonic War so that Young had heard that Champollion had published the first two volumes of his projected monumental work on Egypt, he had not been able to lay his hands on a copy. We can imagine his excitement when he secured a copy from Hudson who had visited Paris during the time Napoleon was in exile on Elba. Young's papers describe how he went through the index of Champollion's work for any reference to the Rosetta inscriptions. He was undoubtedly relieved to find that the volumes included only a few phrases translated from the demotic text and none of the hieroglyphic writing. The only demotic words Champollion claimed to have translated were those de Sacy and Akerblad had already published and he gave no credit to either of them! In fact, Champollion never gave anyone else any credit for being the first in the translation of any Egyptian writing.

Champollion sent the Royal Society a copy of the first two volumes of his *L'Egypte sous les Pharaons*. Young, as Foreign Secretary of the Society, thanked him and wrote to him: "I do not know if by chance M. de Sacy, with whom you are no doubt in contact, has already told you of an example that I have sent him of my translation of the demotic inscription at the beginning of October." [17]

Champollion replied, "M. Silvestre de Sacy, my honored Professor, has not informed me of your memoire on the Egyptian text of the Rosetta inscription; I must tell you Monsieur, how eagerly I shall receive the example that you have the generosity to offer me." [18] Apparently, De Sacy, did not trust Champollion or Champollion was not being honest with Young for he said that de Sacy had not shown him Young's translation of the demotic writing on the Rosetta Stone in May, 1815 although Young had sent it to him the previous October. Young, completely trusting a fellow scholar, sent the memoir to Champollion's brother to give to Champollion.

Eliza was very suspicious of Champollion's behavior. "I hope you're never going to write to that man again," she warned. "Even his own people don't trust him."

Thomas, from his Quaker background was less upset with Champollion's behavior. He was sure that the scholars of the world would eventually acknowledge his own contributions no matter how other people behaved. "He's just a young man," he reasoned soothingly. "He's eager to make a name for himself and sometimes acts foolishly. I am sure that when he has gained a reputation—and his genius with languages will earn him that—he will be less anxious to insist on taking the credit for every advance in Egyptology."

But Eliza was fierce in her protection of her husband and was not ready to go along with his trust in the goodness of his fellow men. "Have you forgotten Lord Brougham and how terribly he treated you?" she sputtered. "How many times do you have to be mistreated before you learn that all men are not as noble as you?"

From the height of his 42 years, Young smiled at Eliza. "When Champollion's genius is recognized," he said, "I'll wager that he gives proper credit to those who proceeded him as all good scholars do." Young was a genius but Eliza was far smarter than he about human beings. Champollion never did give anyone, including Young, any credit for work on the Rosetta Stone that made his later translation possible.

Having translated the demotic part of the Rosetta Stone in one summer during his spare time, Young thought that the translation of the hieroglyphic section would be a "piece of cake". He put the problem on the back burner and only looked at it from time to time when his practice and other projects permitted. A year later he had to admit that the problem was a lot tougher than he thought it would be.

Half of the hieroglyphic message was missing and what remained had too few of the strange characters for him to match it up with either the Greek or the demotic passages. No one knew whether the writing should be read left to right or vice versa. He later showed it can be either, depending on how the animals, birds and people are facing; they always face the beginning of a line. The rules of Egyptian grammar were unknown. Did they write, "He walked to the grand palace which was situated on a hill," as we do in English, or "he walked to the palace grand which was situated on a hill," as the French would? Or perhaps they wrote, "He to the grand palace on a hill situated, walked," as the Germans might have it. They may even have not used words but showed a man walking toward a large building on a hill.

In addition, the Egyptians, we know now, omitted most of the vowels which is also true for wedge-shaped cuneiform and Early Hebrew. In Egyptian, the word "nefer" which means lord or god or good, is written NFR. Nowadays, by convention, Egyptologists put in E's whenever they are not sure which vowel to use. NFR might actually be enfere or other combinations of various vowels with NFR. (Akhenaten, the Sun Pharaoh, was once translated Chanuten!) To complicate matters even further, we now know the Egyptians used symbols which could stand for a single letter, two letters (biliteral) or even three and some of the signs called determinants do not stand for letters at all but give a clue to the subject as a whole. In addition, the Egyptians were logical and liked to put first things first. Unfortunately their first is not always what we would call first. Tut-ankh-amun (King Tut) was usually written Amun-tut-ankh. Amun being a god, came first.

Young knew that after ten years of effort, Champollion still hadn't made any progress in translating the Rosetta Stone so he wasn't too concerned that the Frenchman might beat him to it. What really began to take up a great deal of his time was an amazing spin of the wheel of fortune. After 15 years of neglect, his wave theory of light and his discovery of interference suddenly became the talk of the French Academy of Science. While the British public never took his theory seriously, he became a hero to the French. How did such a turn-about occur?

The Rosetta Stone
courtesy of the British Museum

Young Makes Waves Again

Chapter 19

As Foreign Correspondent for the Royal Society, Young had gotten to know many European scientists. He met some of them personally during visits to France and became close friends with Professor Arago, one of the top astronomers and physicists in the world. Arago was a peppery man who didn't act like a professor at all. He was about five feet, five inches, (the same as Young) which was usual in France after Napoleon's wars had led to the death of a large number of its tall, young men. Arago defended his ideas and attacked his opponents as if they were threatening his life. But a few minutes later, at a nearby cafe, he could be all friendliness and good fellowship over a glass of wine. Young liked him enormously and had sent Arago his papers on light. Arago was impressed and tried to get the most influential scientists in France to read them but they refused to believe Newton could be wrong. The leader of France's scientists at that time was Professor La Place. He absolutely refused to listen to Arago—and then a modern miracle occurred.

A young student named Fresnel came to Arago to show him work he had done which proved that light travels in waves, not as particles. He confessed later that he was deeply disappointed when Arago told him that Young had already done some of this work more than ten years earlier. However, Fresnel was a true gentleman and scientist. After

Thomas Young: Forgotten Genius

reading Young's publications, he wrote to Young that he was adding a note to his own papers, making it clear that Young's work had preceded his. He also pointed out correctly that he had carried Young's ideas much further and with the use of more modern mathematics, he had proved and extended many ideas that Young had only suggested.

Fresnel's papers produced a sensation when they were read before the French Academy and he and Young became the darlings of a large group of French scientists.

During the summer of 1816, shortly after Arago had learned about Fresnel's work, he visited Young at Worthing, accompanied by Gay Lussac, a famous chemist and physicist. They had a lively discussion about how much of Fresnel's work was a repetition of Young's and how much was new. Arago argued that Fresnel had been first to demonstrate that rays which are reflected from a bent surface produce curves of a certain shape. Young was sure that he had demonstrated that in his lectures. The argument got heated (it often did when Arago was excited) and the three men were almost shouting at each other. Eliza, who had been quietly sitting in the room, rose abruptly and walked out. The two Frenchmen were horror-stricken.

"We have offended Madame Young," Arago exclaimed and they wanted to rush out and apologize to her. But in a few moments Eliza reappeared, carrying an enormous volume of Young's lectures. She placed the book on a table, found page 407 and without a word pointed to a graph which showed that Young had calculated what shape beams take when reflected from various curved surfaces. Then she said quietly, "Would you gentlemen like a cup of tea?"

The younger French scientists of the National Academy voted a prize for Fresnel, but some of the older men refused to go along. They refused to admit that Newton (and they) had been wrong. Arago, who brought to science the passion that men usually reserve for love or war, and a man named Biot had been friends but they had a bitter quarrel about Fresnel's and Young's theory of light and never spoke to each other again. Fresnel had to wait nine years after his first paper had been published before he was admitted to the French Academy of Science.

Hudson Gurney and Eliza had tried to get Young to bring his wave theory of light to a larger audience than the small group in England that had accepted it. But Young was convinced that scientists would rediscover his theory and in due time (possibly after his death) he would receive full credit for this important advance. Young fought for recognition for Fresnel in England and was able to have him voted into the Royal Society as a foreign member, which was a great honor. Two years later, as Fresnel was succumbing to tuberculosis at the early age of 39, Young was able to get the Royal Society to award its Rumford Prize to Fresnel. It was delivered shortly before the death of this brilliant and honest scientist.

With the recognition by the French, Young at last felt vindicated in his belief that a person who makes a scientific discovery will be recognized sooner or later by his colleagues. But this was before he encountered Champollion.

Chapter 20

Once he attacked a problem, Young hung on like a bulldog until he had solved it. Even during the time he became famous in France, he continued to attack the translation of the hieroglyphs. However, one problem at a time was not enough to keep his brain busy.

One night Young told Eliza that he had accepted a position on a committee set up by the House of Commons, the Royal Astronomers and the Royal Society to recommend standards of weights and measures that would be uniform throughout England and Scotland.

"Why in the world did you agree to sit on this committee when you are making such slow progress with the Rosetta Stone?" she asked him. "I am afraid Champollion will use your translation of the demotic writing, guess a few hieroglyphic words and claim all of the credit for himself."

"I'm not afraid that Champollion will steal my thunder," Young replied. "I hear from de Sacy that he is running around in circles and getting nowhere. It is very tedious work, translating the demotic writing but I am beginning to see a pattern that I think will lead me to the solution of the hieroglyphic signs. I can't work on the Egyptian writing all of the time and this committee is important. With the growth of science, we must have standards we can rely on."

"Do you realize," he went on, "that our standard yard is

Thomas Young: Forgotten Genius

based on the length of the arm of a king who lived 700 years ago? And our inch until the time of Queen Elizabeth was the average of the length of the thumbs of three men measured from the root of the nail? In this scientific age that is dawning, we must have standards that we can rely on and that can easily be replaced if our standards are ever lost."

The French had set the meter as their standard of length. They claimed it to be 40 millionths of the line from the South to the North Pole that passed through Paris. Obviously nobody ever actually measured this "natural" unit but a bar was scratched and the space between the scratches was taken as a standard meter. Young's committee decided that a yard would be the length of a pendulum that swung back and forth in exactly one second. This is very accurate when the temperature of the air and the height above sea level are known.

After a great deal of discussion and several reports written by Young, it was decided that the pendulum measured 39.13929 inches at 62 degrees Fahrenheit but for practical purposes, a bar with two scratch marks exactly 36 inches apart would be the standard yard. A gallon was defined as the volume occupied by ten pounds of pure water at 62 degrees F. Today, thanks to the use of interferometry to measure tiny distances, the distance between two bands in the wave pattern of pure cadmium are used as a standard unit of length.

Some Weighty Matters

Eliza was well aware that her husband was not being completely candid when he gave his reasons for agreeing to serve as secretary to the Royal Commission on Weights and Measures. They both knew that, as the only true scientist on the Board, he would do most of the committee's work and supply the most fruitful ideas. What Young did not admit was that he had accepted the position at no salary to ease his conscience at having agreed at the same time to serve on the Board of Longitude and Latitude at an annual salary that nearly doubled his income.

For some time, money had been a source of disagreement between Eliza and Thomas. Before he had met her, he realized that the kind of men whose company he enjoyed were the well-educated scholars, clergymen, physicians and men of the business and political worlds who had had classical educations at Cambridge and Oxford Universities. He had been frequently invited to their homes for an evening of good food, stimulating talk and classical music played by professional musicians. He realized that in order to be accepted into this wealthy group, he would have to invite them to his home as well. And his income from his inheritance could not cover such expenses. However, by supplementing from his medical practice, he was able to manage.

When Eliza realized the situation and saw that Thomas was not cut out to be a doctor, she spoke to her father who was a very successful lawyer and she told Thomas just as his uncle had said long before, that he had too rare a mind to waste it merely to earn a living.

"My father would be delighted to establish a fund so that you would not have to waste your beautiful mind simply to make ends meet. I think you'd be wonderfully happy with no patients to distract you from your scientific work. Papa says it would be an honor to him and a pleasure if you would agree."

But Young stubbornly insisted on maintaining his practice and would not think of accepting Mr. Maxwell's generous offer. "I can accept Uncle Brocklesby's money," he argued. "He is no longer alive and it comes from his estate. But money from someone who is still alive would seem like charity to me and I cannot bring myself to accept it."

Eliza appealed to Hudson to change her husband's "old-fashioned" idea but Hudson said, "I have been trying for several years to get him to give up his practice. I even pointed out to him that he could then stop using a pseudonym when publishing his scientific papers and more of the public would know the valuable contributions he has made to science, but he refuses. He is still bound by the strict Quaker philosophy: don't accept help from others if you can manage through your own efforts."

Chapter 21

Having decided that the hieroglyphic message on the Rosetta Stone was too short to form a basis for translation, Young proceeded to collect all of the papyri written in demotic that he could lay his hands on. His intuitive guess was correct: in the end, it was the demotic writing that made it possible for him to crack the hieroglyphic code.

These papyri were very long sheets of writing that were rolled up and placed inside the wrappings of mummies. He painfully translated the demotic writing on the papyri that had been found on mummies from the earliest pharaohs of Egypt down to the most recent. Luckily, they usually mentioned the names of their pharaoh so Young could tell how old they were from known lists of the pharaohs. He found that the messages were prayers to help the dead in the next world. (These prayers are now known as *The Book of the Dead.*)

With his keen eye for minute changes in the script, a habit which he had developed in his youth, he proved his hunch that the demotic writing that scribes used was a simplified form of the hieroglyphic signs so they could write rapidly on the papyrus sheets. In the oldest papyri, the signs looked very similar to the hieroglyphs. They became freer and easier to draw as the Egyptian civilization proceeded down through the centuries.

Thomas Young: Forgotten Genius

He sent a letter to Archduke John of Austria, who was interested in the Rosetta Stone and had visited Young, "I have fully demonstrated the hieroglyphic origin of the running hand (demotic) in which the manuscripts on papyrus, found with the mummies are commonly written...." [19] This letter was circulated to scholars in London, Paris and elsewhere.

Having become expert at deciphering demotic writing, Young felt that he was about ready to tackle hieroglyphic picture writing. One question still bothered him. Did the Egyptians use letters, symbols or a combination of both? At first he (and Champollion) had thought the hieroglyphic writing had no letters, only symbols. However, he saw a resemblance between the uses of hieroglyphic signs and Chinese ideograms. Since the ideograms represented symbols and ideas, he wondered how the Chinese wrote foreign words and names which had no equivalent in Chinese. He already knew some Chinese and, without batting an eye, proceeded to teach himself enough more of the language to learn that when they had to write a foreign word or name, each sign represented a sound (like our alphabetical letters). Now he was ready to search for foreign names in the Rosetta inscription.

The idea had been advanced some years previously that a group of signs surrounded by an oval called a cartouche signified that the name of an important person was enclosed, but the idea had been buried in obscure publications. Young reinvented this old idea (he claimed not to have known it before) and knew from the Greek version of the Stone that Ptolemy should be mentioned several times. He decided that there was a cartouche which contained the letters which spelled "Ptolemy" (Ptolemaios in Greek). There is no question that this is the first hieroglyphic word ever to be translated. Young then translated the name Berenice, a Queen of one of the Ptolemies, which appeared in a different inscription, helped by the fact that he had already figured out that a semicircle with the flat side down meant that the subject was a female. To cap his success and convince him that he was really on the right track, he had the great satisfaction of learning that an amateur Egyptologist, Mr. Bankes, had translated the name Cleopatra from an obelisk (a huge upright stone that looks like a needle), using nine of the letters in Ptolemy and Berenice which he had learned from Young and the semicircle which showed the subject was a female. In a supplement to the *Encyclopedia Britannica*, published in 1819, Young listed 200 hieroglyphic signs he had translated and how to read numbers. If he had taken the trouble to have it printed as a separate publication with a much wider distribution on the Continent, Champollion's claim for priority in translating hieroglyphic writing might never have occurred.

Portrait of Thomas Young, by Sir Thomas Lawrence

courtesy of David Gurney

Enough is Not Enough

Chapter 22

By 1818 Young felt that he had solved the hieroglyphic puzzle by showing that the demotic and hieroglyphic signs were related. He had determined nine letters of the hieroglyphic alphabet and had deciphered more than 200 signs for gods and other words. He knew that Champollion or anyone else who studied his translation of the *Book of the Dead* which was written in demotic, could go on from there to translate all the ancient inscriptions on the monuments and temples of Egypt. He never lost interest in this fascinating language and was actually proof-reading a dictionary of hieroglyphic words—the first ever—on the day he died in 1829. There were several other activities, however, that this untiring man got involved in during this time.

In 1771 the *Encyclopedia Britannica* had been started by two men in Edinburgh. The first edition consisted of three volumes and was said by the publisher to contain authoritative and complete biographies of all the important scholars and scientists living and dead as well as an accurate description of their work. By 1810 three more editions had appeared and the Encyclopedia had expanded to 20 volumes. A new editor, Mcvey Napier, began to assemble a team of scholars to continue this valuable publication. Napier was anxious to expand the number of articles and biographies in scientific areas and everyone he knew told him that Young was the man he needed. In 1814 he appealed to Young for help with the *Fifth Edition*. Young, who had published non-medical articles under a pseudonym for fear that his patients would be upset at the time he spent away from medicine, wrote that the idea appealed to him but he declined to join the list of contributors. Napier's letter had reached him at Worthing during the summer when he was translating the demotic portion of the Rosetta Stone. Two years later, with Napier still interested, Young changed his mind and agreed to co-operate provided his articles appeared under a pseudonym. Napier, the editor, asked which topics Young could write on authoritatively. Young astounded him by offering to write on: alphabet, annuities, attraction, capillary action, cohesion, color, dew, Egypt, the eye, focus, friction, halo, hieroglyphic, hydraulics, motion, resistance, ship, sound, tides, waves and anything medical. What an imposing list of subjects for any one person to be able to write on with authority! There will probably never again be a time when one person can pull off such a feat.

Some of these topics were already promised by others but Young was asked to write on 16 subjects with his own illustrations and 45 biographies totaling about 380 pages. The other contributors wrote one or two subjects or biographies but Napier tried to get this human encyclopedia to take on any subject for which he couldn't locate an expert. Most encyclopedia authors present a review of a subject. Young's articles not only reviewed a topic but often contained new, original ideas as well.

His article, "Bridge," astounded one of the leading bridge builders of London, Mr. Rennie, by the depth of the knowledge and the new ideas it contained. Rennie tried to find out from Napier who "O.R." (Young's pseudonym) was. He wrote that "when separated, O.R. stands for two contributors to the encyclopedia, but their combined strength could not have produced the 'Bridge'." The article on carpentry developed what is known today as "Young's Modulus of Elasticity" which is still taught to physics students and engineers. It describes the forces acting on supporting beams and how tests can be carried out to determine how much load a beam can support. An article on cohesion considers the curved surface (meniscus) of a liquid in a narrow tube. He showed that forces tend to act on liquids in a narrow tube (capillary action). This pull is determined by the shape of the tube and the pull of gravity against the forces which hold molecules together.

The article on road building is of interest to us today because he described the ideas of a man named Loudon McAdams who had suggested improvements in road construction and the materials used. We use his name for the tarry substance, macadam, which is widely employed today to pave roads.

Young also broke new ground with his article on tides.

Thomas Young: Forgotten Genius

Newton had applied his laws of gravity to explain how the moon and the sun cause tides. However, he treated the water on the earth as if it played no part in affecting the tides. Young showed how the oscillation of the water in the seas under the pull of the sun and moon set up pendulum-like swings. When this factor is taken into account, it is much easier to explain the heights of tides in different parts of England and elsewhere.

His articles on weights and measures and on Egypt as we already know were major contributions.

Somehow, in addition to writing for the *Encyclopedia* and working on hieroglyphs, Young found time to serve on a committee formed by the Admiralty to evaluate a new method of building warships. A master shipbuilder named Robert Sepping had discovered a way to examine the keels and the bottoms of ships which were in dry-dock. He found that many of the timbers had been loosened and cracked during launching or during storms in the North Sea. Sepping felt that when a ship was on top of a wave, the front and rear ends (bow and stern) were up in the air and their weight put an enormous strain on the middle of the ship, sometimes actually breaking the beams. This arching of a ship was called "logging." He suggested that the boards which came out at right angles from the keel to form the bottom of the ships should be braced with diagonal beams; instead of forming rectangles, diagonal braces would form triangles. If you place a wooden box on its side and press down on it, the sides of the box will move and the corners will become loose and no longer form right angles. This cannot happen with a triangle; the sides cannot move. Sepping received a medal and money for this idea and the Secretary of the Head of the Admiralty, Sir John Barrow, became an enthusiastic supporter of Sepping's ideas which included changing the shape of the ships so that the front end was narrow instead of round which would improve efficiency and save a large amount of timber.

Sepping was allowed to try his ideas on two warships that were docked for repairs. After ten years at sea the ships were examined and the results were exactly as Seppings had predicted. It was impossible for Sir John Barrow to order such a huge change in the Navy without strong support, so he convened a committee of which Young was the secretary (and did most of the work) to give a scientific opinion of the value of Seppings' ideas.

Young accepted reluctantly. He preferred theoretical problems but felt it was his duty to do what he could for the sailors whose lives were involved. He soon found that he was in the middle of a big controversy. The Committee's report, which supported Sepping's ideas, pleased nobody. The older shipbuilders did not know much theoretical science and did not want any changes in ship construction. They apparently felt that the British navy had defeated the Spanish

Thomas Young: Forgotten Genius

Armada and no changes were needed even though that battle had been fought more than 200 years earlier. The Admirals were against changing the bow of the ships from rounded to slim because this would have removed a luxurious lounge that they didn't want to give up. The Admirals were pragmatic men who did not believe that inexperienced landlubbers knew what sailing was all about. One Admiral wrote to Young and the Committee, "Though science is much respected by their Lordships and your paper is much esteemed, it is too learned." Sir John Barrow, who favored the proposal, was upset because he thought the report was not strong enough. Even though it supported Seppings, he had hoped for a resounding endorsement to override the opposition of the shipbuilders and the Admirals. Young, in his scientific way, had cited all of the uncertainties involved and the final report while it agreed with Seppings, sounded half-hearted to Barrow. However, the report carried the day and for the next 50 years, until ironclad ships were built during the American Civil War, British warships were reinforced with diagonal beams along their bottoms and the Admirals had to do without their large recreation room.

Chapter 23

After his supplement to the *Encyclopedia Britannica* on Egypt appeared in 1819, Young could sit back and wait for the honors to roll in. He was the only person in the world who had published any advances in translating ancient Egyptian since de Sacy and Akerblad had made a slight beginning many years before. He felt confident that his work provided the guideposts that would enable others to continue down the road he had laid out. Eliza realized that this was the moment, if there ever was one, when she should bring up an idea that had been on her mind for a long time.

"Thomas," she said to him one evening, "we've stopped going to Worthing for our summer vacations and I've been thinking about interesting things we could do together. When you were a student in Gottingen, you traveled around but you weren't able to go to Italy, France, Switzerland or southern Germany because of the French wars. Now would be a good time for us to take such a trip. And think of the amusement you would have planning our route and making the arrangements."

"You've always wanted to see the art galleries in Rome and Florence," she continued, "and you could drop a heavy and a light object from the Tower of Pisa and see for yourself if Galileo was right. You've always said you want to see other people's results with your own eyes," she teased him.

She could see that he was tempted. Young had always had a streak in him that led him to music, dancing and other forbidden pleasures in spite of his early Quaker upbringing. However, knowing his strong work habits, she realized that it seemed almost wicked to him to break off from his work and just have a good time.

Wisely, she went on, "You told me just the other day that there are some Egyptian manuscripts in Italy that you'd like to make copies of. The French Academy has been begging you to come for a visit, and in Paris we could see Arago, Fresnel and other scientists. You haven't any deadlines to meet right now and there are no wars on the Continent. Oh, Thomas, what fun we'd have!"

"You've taken away all my objections," he smiled at her. "How can I say anything but yes?"

"There's something else about a visit to the Continent," she went on happily. "You and I have not talked about having no children but I know it is often on our minds. I am only 38 and perhaps a change of scenery and the two of us together without the distractions of your other activities might make a difference. You speak of your puzzles as if they are your children but I for one want to see your valuable mind carried on into the future."

And so they took a grand tour through much of Europe but sadly, they had no children.

The Grand Tour

Near the end of the tour, they received word that Eliza's mother was very sick. Before they could sail back to England, she died at the Maxwell home on Tibbenden Lane in Farnborough, Kent. Young was sorry he could not see her before she passed away. He had gotten very fond of Eliza's parents, her three sisters to whom he wrote often and her brother who was in the Royal Navy. Although he kept contact with his own numerous brothers and sisters, he felt so much a part of the Maxwell family that he told Eliza that when he died he wanted to be buried in the Maxwell family vault at St. Giles Church in Farnborough.

They had hurried to Paris but since they could not get to Mrs. Maxwell's funeral in time, stayed for an meeting of scientists that had been called by the French Academy of Sciences. Young had the chance to re-meet some of his old friends such as Arago and Fresnel and for the first time, he met Champollion. According to Eliza, their meeting was cordial and Young offered Champollion any help he might request in his future work. Champollion thanked him and told him how useful Young's work had been to him and how he agreed with almost all of Young's translations. (Young did not know that Champollion had just written a paper saying that Young was all wrong and that the Egyptian writing did not contain any letters but consisted only of symbols!)

Eliza and Thomas returned to England and settled down

Thomas Young: Forgotten Genius

to what they thought would be a busy but quiet existence. He was nearing 50 and they no longer left London to spend their summers at Worthing. Neither of them cared for country life and they left the city only to visit friends who lived nearby or to spend some time with Hudson Gurney in Norfolk.

About this time he wrote to Hudson:

"I fell into a sort of fidgetty languor [without much energy] and thought I was growing old. It soon wore off, however, and I am convinced there is no better cure for being out of sorts than keeping busy. This autumn I have finished an article on Celestial Mechanics with much difficult mathematics and am re-writing my article on Languages for the *Encyclopaedia Britannica*. I am also preparing a biography of LaGrange which requires a list of 100 papers. I, of course, have the business of the Board of Longitude and the Royal Society and I must attend my private patients. Then I must not forget that I must shortly do a little more to the hieroglyphics." Clearly Young expected that his life would now be busy but uneventful. He had not, however, reckoned on the shock that Champollion was preparing for him.

Chapter 24

What had Champollion accomplished between 1810 and 1819 when Young's breakthrough was published in the *Encyclopedia Britannica*? With a shrewd eye toward publicity, he had published the first two volumes of what were to be *the* definitive works on Ancient Egypt and staked his claim to being the foremost scholar in this field. He had maintained a large correspondence in which he kept referring to progress he was making in translating the Rosetta Stone, but he had not published a word of the Egyptian writing on the Rosetta Stone or elsewhere. We now know that he had gotten nowhere because he had made a wrong turn and had found himself in a blind alley. He completely rejected the idea that any of the hieroglyphs could represent a letter of the alphabet. In fact, he published a paper in 1821 in which he claimed to have disproved scholars (including Young) who thought the inscriptions contained alphabetic letters along with signs. In this paper he said two important things. First, he claimed to have discovered that the demotic writing is only a simple modification of the hieroglyphic system and second, the demotic characters (and also the hieroglyphic) are "signs of things and not signs of sounds"; in other words, the Egyptian writing does not have alphabetical letters.

It is difficult to understand how Champollion, five years

after Young had announced that the demotic writing was derived from the hieroglyphic, could claim the credit for this observation. Champollion, like Lord Brougham, seemed confident that educated people who were not experts on Egypt, would not know that Young had already published this important fact.

What caused Champollion to wake up and realize that the hieroglyphs *did* contain alphabetical letters? We now know that his complete about face occurred immediately after he received a copy of a letter from Bankes who had translated the name Cleopatra from an obelisk using Young's letters from Ptolemy and Berenice. It seems very possible that Champollion applied Young's letters from the three names to other inscriptions and found that Young's system worked—he was able to recognize the names of several Roman rulers. [20] He immediately tried to recapture all of the copies of his paper from the select group to whom he had sent it, in order to destroy it. Fortunately, a few copies were not returned and escaped destruction so we could learn the true story. Champollion then recirculated only that part of the article which claimed he had discovered the derivation of the demotic from the hieroglyphic signs. He removed the date from the article and erased his claim that the Egyptian writing did not use an alphabet.

Then, in 1822, less than one year later, Champollion published a letter which made him famous. He took full credit for having solved both the demotic and the hieroglyphic writing of the ancient Egyptians. Akerblad, de Sacy and Young were dismissed as minor and often misguided writers in the field. He did not deny that Young was the first to translate any hieroglyphic words—he simply ignored it. In an incredibly short time after he had learned that Young was on the right track, he had established a large vocabulary, a beginning grasp of the grammar and syntax of the language and had translated many passages of the Rosetta Stone and other inscriptions. Overnight, Champollion, who had been known to only a small group of scholars, became famous throughout the western world as French newspapers proclaimed "Brilliant French Scholar Translates Ancient Egyptian Language" or similar headlines. He suddenly emerged from obscurity, poverty and neglect into the bright sunshine of public and royal acclaim. Even the King of France summoned him for an audience.

Champollion never did explain how he succeeded in translating the hieroglyphs when just a few months before he had stated that they were not phonetic and did not contain alphabetical letters. He wrote in 1822 that he had succeeded in translating the hieroglyphs by discovering that the demotic writing was derived from the priestly signs and by utilizing his knowledge of Chinese! (The coincidence of this approach to Young's, which had been published several years before seems too striking to be chance.) He, of course, never mentioned anybody else's work, including Bankes' translation of Cleopatra which Champollion claimed he had translated using almost the exact reasoning Bankes had used and had explained in the letter he had sent to Champollion.

Although Young wished Champollion well and offered his help to the Frenchman, Champollion had other ideas. He maintained a polite manner in his letters to Young and spoke of sharing knowledge with him but history shows he did otherwise. A papyrus, which was a bill of sale written in demotic, fell into Champollion's hands. On the reverse side was an endorsement with several Greek names. On a visit to Paris by Young, Champollion gave him a copy of the bill of sale "to help him with his research," but did not include the Greek names on the back. By a coincidence worthy of Dickens, a friend of Young's while in Thebes in Egypt bought a copy of the same bill of sale with the Greek names on the back and gave it to Young. Young realized that the two papyri were the same and he wrote to Champollion asking for a copy of the Greek endorsement on the back. He never received a response from Champollion. In his typical fashion, Young mused in a letter to Gurney: "He perhaps thought it best for me to try my strength upon the original without any assistance which might have been derived from it with respect to two or three of the names." [21]

Young finally lost his controlled manner, however, when Champollion refused to give him any credit at all and belittled or ignored his contributions. The title of the article he wrote to set the record straight leaves no doubt about the less than Brotherly nature of his feelings—"An Account of Some Recent Discoveries in Hieroglyphical Literature and Egyptian Antiquities with the Author's Original Alphabet as extended by Mr. Champollion." And this time he published it under his own name.

For a number of years after Young's death in 1829 and Champollion's in 1832, a fierce debate raged as to who should receive credit for translating the Egyptian hieroglyphic writing. The English, led by George Peacock and a number of Scottish scholars, felt that Young had clear priority in the field although they granted that Champollion's contributions were immense while the French, particularly Jean-Jacques Champollion-Figeac, Champollion's older brother, claimed the entire honor for their countryman and allowed Young no credit whatsoever. When his friend Arago asked Young why he did not respond to the arguments about priority in the translation of the hieroglyphic writing, Young wrote:

"I thought M. Champollion had been unjust to me, but I freely forgave him, without requiring him to acknowledge his injustice....The true foundation of the analysis of the Egyptian system, I insist is the fact of the original identity of the [demotic] with the [hieroglyphic] which I discovered and printed in 1816, and which M. Champollion probably rediscovered and certainly republished in 1821; besides [there is] the reading of the name of Ptolemy, which I had completely ascertained and published in 1814, and the name of Cleopatra, which Mr. Bankes had afterwards discovered by means of the information that I sent out to Egypt, and which he asserts he communicated indirectly to M. Champollion." [22]

In spite of Young's refusal to make known the unsavory tricks Champollion had pulled on an unsuspecting public, he might still have gained some credit for his pioneering work if politics had not also intervened. The French had been beaten by Nelson at Trafalgar and then crushed by Wellington at Waterloo. Morale in France was at rock bottom when Champollion's claim to fame hit the headlines. He immediately became a national hero. French pride was reborn and it became almost a patriotic duty to proclaim him as the greatest scholar in the world. For a Frenchman to support Young's claim was almost the equivalent of treason.

One of the first to join the wildly cheering French crowd was de Sacy—the same man who had described Champollion to Young as a charlatan! Even Arago came out in favor of Champollion when he became convinced that Champollion's approach was more comprehensive than Young's. Young refused to challenge Champollion's claims in the daily newspapers but, in response to a French writer, he came close to losing his temper. In a burst of sarcasm he wrote:

"[In 1821] Akerblad was dead; Champollion had not *then* done anything worth mentioning on the subject of hieroglyphics. I had published, *seven years* before, and had sent directly to Champollion, a literal translation of the two inscriptions on the Pillar of Rosetta: I had sent the name of Ptolemy and the interpretation of many other characters to the English travellers in Egypt; it was *after* my return from Italy that Champollion received the name of Cleopatra, as ascertained in Egypt by Mr. Bankes from my letters; it is hence that he himself dates the origin of his system: Ergo opera illius mea sunt! (Therefore, his works are mine!)" [23]

If Champollion had been the least bit generous and had admitted publicly that Young had translated the demotic portion of the Rosetta Stone and in his Encyclopedia article in 1819 had published the first translation of any hieroglyphic word (Ptolemy), there would still have been plenty of credit for his own brilliant work from 1822 until his untimely death in 1832.

For many years, even after Champollion's death, Peacock had been pushing Young's case vigorously and in particular he openly charged that Champollion had written that the hieroglyphic language had no alphabet. The Frenchman had called in the article and had re-issued it with the date and his glaring error removed when he had learned that Young's alphabetic letters enabled Mr. Bankes to translate Cleopatra from a monument. Peacock was joined in the argument by Heinrich Klaproth, a distinguished professor on Oriental Languages in Paris who had been born in Berlin. He had been suspicious of Champollion's honesty and had kept a copy of the article Champollion had tried to recall and destroy. He claimed that for ten years people had been talking enthusiastically about the discovery of the phonetic alphabet made by the late M. Champollion, but few people seemed to have had any clear idea of what it really was "...Dr. Young, in England, was beyond contradiction the first author of this discovery. The idea that the hieroglyphs could contain an alphabet section never took root in Champollion's mind," Klaproth wrote.

Champollion's older brother in a letter to the Director of the *Revue Britannique*, offered his rebuttal to Peacock's charges. His arguments would be considered a masterpiece of double-talk by a writer today who is forced to answer a serious charge when he knows the charge is true: he ignored the serious charge and went to great lengths to explain minor points! [24]

1. How could Peacock say that the French were prejudiced against Young, he asked, when they had paid him the rare tribute of election to the exclusive French Academy of Science? (He didn't mention that this was for Young's work on the wave theory of light.)

2. He claimed that Champollion knew nothing of Young's work before 1822 even though Young had sent him

many letters and samples of his translations before this time.

3. He did not answer Peacock's (and Klaproth's) charge that Champollion only a few months before his "breakthrough," had published a paper stating that the Egyptian language had no alphabet and had called back and destroyed the originals. Instead, he said that contrary to Peacock's and Klaproth's charges, his brother had made no attempt to suppress this article. The article can be found in the Imperial Library in Paris, he stated, and Klaproth, who had claimed the article had been suppressed by Champollion had two copies in his own library. This was "a malevolent invention of the Prussian Klaproth," he charged. He offered no explanation how his brother came to realize that he was in a blind alley!

4. He claimed that his brother had translated the hieroglyph for the sign meaning "worship" in 1810 but had not gotten around to publishing it!

5. He did not mention that Champollion had drawn up a list of his publications before his death in which the article claiming the hieroglyphs had no alphabetic representation does not appear.

6. Finally, he did not see how anyone could claim that his brother had mistreated the Englishman when Young's letters to Champollion were unfailingly friendly and polite.

The scale was tipped in favor of Champollion when Lepsius, a brilliant Egyptologist, decided that the output of

Thomas Young: Forgotten Genius

the Frenchman far outweighed the few papers by Young. One important aspect of the argument is often overlooked by Young's supporters. Even with the alphabet that Young was working out, the letters were only useful in translating the proper names of important dignitaries—usually in a cartouche—and other proper nouns. Translating the hieroglyphic sign into English letters still did not explain what the inscriptions were saying. Perhaps this is why Lepsius decided that Champollion deserved the lion's share of the credit even though Young was the first to make any progress at all and Champollion's accomplishments stemmed directly from the leads he got from Young's work.

To this day the argument still is revived from time to time by scholars who do not feel it is correct for Champollion to receive all the credit for translating the hieroglyphic writing of the Rosetta Stone. In 1986 the British Museum published a new booklet on the Rosetta Stone by Carol Andrews. Young's contribution is made clear but textbooks and teachers still give all of the credit to Champollion.

Last But Not Least

Chapter 25

Now in his 50's, Young slowed his activities down to what others might call a busy schedule. Besides continuing to work on Egyptian translations and articles and biographies for the Encyclopedia Britannica, he agreed to serve as Secretary of the Board of Longitude and Superintendent of its publication, the *Nautical Almanac*. This Board was responsible for publishing a yearly almanac that had up-to-date astronomical information to help sailors determine exactly where they were (on cloudless nights) from the positions of the moon, the stars, the visible planets and the moons of Jupiter. Young wasn't too excited by this position but it carried a good salary and even more important to him, it was a useful activity that would help sailors and prevent the loss of lives at sea.

Unfortunately, before Young took over the publication of the *Almanac*, errors had begun to appear and criticism of the *Almanac* was widespread. Young quickly corrected the errors but he in turn became the object of strong criticism from astronomers who wanted more information about the stars in the *Almanac* even though the information would not be useful to navigators. Young took the position that the proper place for astronomical data was in the Proceedings of the Royal Society, not in the *Almanac*. A bitter quarrel resulted with a Mr. Baily, an astronomer, that continued for the rest of Young's life.

Young could easily have included the data the astronomers wanted in the Almanac but he refused. He said the Almanac was for practical navigation not theoretical astronomers—an unexpected position for a man to take who had supported science for its own sake all his life. It is possible that he really resisted Mr. Baily because the Royal Society was being somewhat neglected at this stage of its history and he wanted more scientists to take an interest in its activities and publications.

In addition to publishing the *Nautical Almanac*, the Board of Longitude had money in its budget to offer prizes for any advances that would be useful to sailors or to England. Large sums were offered for better ways to determine the position of a ship, day or night. There were also prizes for ships that could find a northern passage from the Atlantic to the Pacific. The further west a ship explored within the Arctic Circle, the greater the prize. Young became convinced that there was no water passage between the two oceans but he felt the prizes were worthwhile because better maps were made possible and large sightings of whales were noted which helped whalers. (At that time whale oil was prized to fill British lamps. Gas lighting had been introduced into London a few years earlier but was not yet widely available.)

In 1826, Eliza and Thomas moved into a new house that

they had helped to design. Two years later he received the rare honor of being elected one of only eight foreign associates of the French Academy of Sciences. Volta, the Italian physicist, had died earlier that year so that another appointment could be made to make up the eight foreigners allowed. He and Eliza went to Paris for the initiation ceremony. Champollion was now being acclaimed as the hero of the cracking of the hieroglyphic code but Young did not quarrel with him about his lack of generosity, not to say honesty, in refusing to admit Young's priority. He felt confident that scholars in the future would recognize his earlier publications and give him all the credit that was due to him.

Hudson Gurney felt that Young would be recognized some day as one of the greatest scientists and scholars England had ever produced. He and Eliza arranged to have Young's portrait painted by Sir Thomas Lawrence, London's foremost portrait painter. Copies of the portrait are located at The Royal Society and St. George's Hospital in London, at Emmanuel College at Cambridge and the original is in the possession of a descendent of Hudson Gurney.

Young continued working at his usual pace until February, 1829. He then began to suffer from severe asthmatic attacks, the same ailment that his uncle Brockelsby had treated him for when he was 17. Now, however, he began to suffer from greater and greater weakness. His mind remained clear and he completed an Egyptian-English dictionary. He kept busy proof-reading its pages and making corrections with a pencil because he could no longer hold a pen. Hudson thought Thomas was over-tiring himself and wanted him to stop working but Young said that it didn't fatigue him but was an amusement.

A few people were still attacking him because of his handling of the *Nautical Almanac* but when some of his friends wrote a rebuttal, he asked them not to publish it since it would only increase the irritation of all concerned.

Early in April, Young realized that his illness was not going to improve when his coughing began to bring up blood. He faced his death with remarkable calmness. He invited his closest friends for final visits and, of course, Hudson was there daily.

"Hudson," he had written to his friend when he first realized his illness was serious, "I don't think my health would have been any worse if I had been less rigid in my daily habits. But if I had my life to live over again, there is little that I would want to do differently. After all these years, I feel content to know that there are only two things that I never learned which I might wish to have learned early in life; when to get up and when to go to bed." [25]

"In the very last stage of his illness, his self-possession was most remarkable," said his biographer and friend, George Peacock. "In our last conversation, after some personal comments and some instructions concerning the hieroglyphic papers he had just finished proof-reading, he said that whether he ever partially recovered or was rapidly taken off, he could patiently and contentedly wait; he had settled all of his responsibilities; if his health had continued, he would have liked to do more of what he had so enjoyed in the past but even though he was not suffering any pain, only weakness, if his life continued so that he couldn't resume his usual activities, he did not wish his dying to be prolonged." [26]

In the morning of May 10, 1829 he died peacefully, having lived 56 of the most productive years of any man on earth. At his earlier request, an autopsy was performed for the benefit of science and it was found that his aorta, (which carries blood away from the heart), was almost completely blocked.

Eliza, with Hudson Gurney's assistance, had arranged to have a sculptor prepare a bust of Young from a cast that was made immediately after his death. The cast wasn't perfect, however, so a profile was carved on a plaque from Lawrence's portrait. An inscription on the slab beneath the profile was written by Hudson Gurney. The plaque was accepted by the Dean of Westminster Abbey to be placed among the previous great men of England where Hudson and Eliza felt it belonged and where it can be seen today.

Thomas Young: Forgotten Genius

Plaque in Westminister Abbey

photograph by Vivian Kline

Chapter 26

On May 29, 1839, Eliza and George Peacock, met at dinner with Hudson Gurney and Mag to commemorate the tenth anniversary of Young's death. After the dinner dishes had been removed, Mag set the tone for the small gathering.

"If Thomas were here, he would want singing, dancing and laughter. He had his serious side, of course, and wherever he now may be, he would be pleased that we remember his scientific accomplishments but he would not want us to become sentimental or lugubrious this evening," she declared firmly.

"I could not agree with you more," Eliza chimed in. "I wish I knew enough Latin or Greek to make one of his classical puns. I know that's what he'd do. I have some news for all of you," she went on. "I have decided to take up my sister Emily's offer to live with her and her husband in Warwickshire. It will be difficult for me to leave the house on Park Square that Thomas and I had built to our own specifications and lived in only three years together but it makes little sense for me to maintain such a large establishment with a doctor's office and reception room and his large laboratory. I've found a few more notes and letters, George," she said to Peacock. "These should complete all of Thomas' papers for his biography. How is it progressing?"

"I must confess that I was shocked to realize that ten

years have already gone by since his death," Peacock admitted, "and I still have a great deal of his life to describe. When I was invited to this dinner party, I was reminded of how little recognition his work has gained in the past ten years. Perhaps he was so far ahead of his contemporaries that it will take time for them to realize how remarkable his ideas were."

"I think you're partly correct, George," Eliza joined in, "but I cannot overlook the fact that three famous men treated Thomas abominably. Dr. Home denied him the credit for proving that the lens in the eye is responsible for near and far vision, and that beast, Lord Brougham, turned the world's attention from Thomas' proof that light travels in waves and useful interference patterns form, until the French forced the truth down his throat. He still has not apologized publicly. And, of course, Champollion never gave Thomas any credit for showing him how to attack the Rosetta Stone successfully. To this day, Champollion's brother will not admit that his younger brother denied that the hieroglyphic language has an alphabet until he saw Thomas' results. I wonder if any other scientist ever encountered three such ungenerous individuals?

"He certainly was badly treated by those egotistical men," Hudson agreed. "I am sure they took advantage of him knowing that his response would be that of a gentleman. However, I think he might still have become a scientist known to every British schoolboy if he had published under his own name instead of using a pseudonym most of his life. I wanted to publicize his work beyond the small group of knowledgeable readers of the Royal Society publications and the other highly specialized journals he wrote for, but I couldn't as long as he did not use his own name. He said that he didn't want his patients to know how much time he spent outside of his practice but I think they would have felt just the opposite if he had gained the attention that was due to him. I wrote his memoirs and hoped he would get the recognition he deserved but it never reached a wide public. I think that my close friendship with Thomas which goes back so many years entitles me to venture a comment which I hope you will all take in the open spirit with which I offer it. I believe that underneath his Quaker modesty was a fierce pride in himself. He turned down my ideas of making his discoveries widely known because he felt that his work would someday be recognized for its own merits and he thought scientists should not stoop to what he felt was personal advertisement."

"I suppose that if Thomas had not chosen to work alone but had some young students as Arago had with Fresnel, such followers would have carried his researches on and would be reminding the scientific world of his seminal discoveries," Peacock ventured. "I think you all know that I advised him not to jump so quickly from one subject to the

Thomas Young: Forgotten Genius

next. He answered that he thought there were two kinds of scientists: those who answered questions with intuitive leaps and those who stayed in one field and consolidated a new finding with many experiments. He felt that there was need for both types and he believed he had the kind of mind that needed fresh problems to solve rather than remaining in a new field that he had discovered and studying it in depth. I think that it hurts his reputation today that he plowed many fields but did not dig deeply. When textbooks are written or scholars write histories of a subject, they mention a few people who did early work in a field or advanced new ideas but the ones who put the new ideas on a solid basis are the names that are remembered.

"How many of us educated people around this table, besides me since I am a scientist, have any idea who the important scientists of today are? We were taught Latin and Greek and read the classics but I had to learn about science myself. It was not in the curriculum. Scientists are rarely mentioned in our newspapers and popular magazines except for a towering figure like Newton. Science is just a young child today but I predict that in the near future it will have such an important role in our lives that every school child will know the names of the important scientists of the day. I have little doubt that if Thomas had lived a few years later, with his many accomplishments, his name would be known to every educated person. He was just too far ahead of his time."

The friends looked at each other for a minute and then Eliza rose. "Whatever people in the future may think of him," she said, "I wish to propose a toast to one of the greatest scientists and scholars that England has ever known and, as you will agree, a wonderful human being," raising her glass, she said proudly, "To Thomas Young!"

St. Giles Church—Burial Place of Thomas Young
Photograph by Vivian Kline

ENDNOTES

[1] George Peacock, *Life of Thomas Young* (London: 1855) 3.

[2] Alexander Wood, *Thomas Young, Natural Philospher* (Completed by Frank Oldham), (London: Cambridge Univ. Press, 1954) 21.

[3] *Journal of Thomas Young*, cited by Peacock, p. 108

[4] G.M. Trevelyan, *Social History of England*, p.366.

[5] Alexander Wood, *Op. cit.*, 72

[6] *Encyclopaedia Britannica*, 11th Ed., (New York: Encyc. Brit. Co.) 1911.

[7] *Edinburgh Review*, Vol. 1, 450.

[8] *Ibid*, Vol. 1, 103.

[9] *Philosophical Trans*. (London), Vol. 92, 12, 1802.

[10] *Nature*, (London: 1934), Vol. 133, 276.

[11] Frank Oldham, *Life of Thomas Young, M.D., F.R.S.*,(London: Arnold & Co., 1933) 76.

[12] *Ibid*, 77.

[13] G. Peacock, and J. Leitch, *Works of the Late Thomas Young*, (London: 1855) Vol. III, 610-611.

[14] Alexander Wood, *Op. cit.*, 210-211

[15] E. A. Wallis Budge, *The Mummy*, (New York: Causeway Books, 1974 (my translation), 133.

[16] *Ibid*, 134. (my translation)

[17] *Ibid*, 137. (my translation)

[18] *Ibid*, 137. (my translation)

[19] *Ibid*, 138. (my translation)

[20] Carol Andrews, *The Rosetta Stone*, (New York: Bedrick, 1988) 27-28.)

[21] Alexander Wood, *Op. Cit.*, 229-230.

[22] *Letter*, Young to Arago, July, 1828.

[23] Alexander Wood, *Op. cit.*, 243.

[24] J. J. Champollion-Figeac, *Letter to Revue Britannique*, (Paris, 1857).

[25] George Peacock and J. Leitch, *Op. cit.*, Vol 3, 449

[26] *Ibid*, 481.

SOURCES

Biographies:

Oldham, Frank. *Thomas Young, Philosopher and Physician*. London: Arnold & Co., 1933.

Peacock, George. *Life of Dr. Thomas Young, M.D., F.R.S.*. London: W. Clowes & sons, 1855.

Wood, Alexander (completed by Frank Oldham). *Thomas Young, Natural Philosopher*. Cambridge: Cambridge University Press, 1954.

Short Biographies:

Bence-Jones, Henry. *The Royal Institution*. New York: Arno Press, 1975.

Deacon William. *Milverton*. Milverton: Milverton Historical Society, 1988.

Gurney, Hudson. *Memoir of the Life of Thomas Young, M.D. F.R.S. in Biographical Memoirs of Celebrated Physicians*. London: Whittaker, 1839.

Biographies in Encyclopedias:

Asimov, Isaac. *Thomas Young in Biographical Encyclopedia of Science & Technology*. Garden City: Doubleday, 1964.

C. H. L. *Thomas Young in Dictionary of National Biography Vol 21*. Oxford: Oxford University Press, 1949.

Thomas Young: Forgotten Genius

Morse, Edgar W., *Thomas Young in Dictionary of Scientific Biography*. New York: Scribner, 1970.

Talbott, John H. *Thomas Young in A Biographical History of Medicine*. New York: Grune & Stratton, 1970.

Most Important Publications of Thomas Young:

Peacock, George and Leitch, John. *Miscellaneous Works of the Late Thomas Young, M.D., F.R.S.* London: 1855.

Young, Thomas. *A Course in Lectures on Natural Philosophy and the Mechanical Arts*. London: 1807, New York: J. Murray, 1971.

Young Thomas. *An Introduction to Medical Literature*. London: Blacks, Underwood & Co., 1813.

Young, Thomas. *Egypt in Encyclopaedia Britannica, Vol. 4*. Edinburgh: George Ramsey & Co., 1819.

Other:

Anderson, Verily. *Friends and Relations*. London: Hodder & Stoughton, 1980.

Andrews, Carol. *Rosetta Stone*. New York: Peter Bedrick, 1988.

Champollion-Figeac, J. J. *Letter* to the Director of *The Revue Britannique*. Paris: Dondey-Dupre, 1857.

Friends Library, Euston Road, London.

SOURCES

Hilts, Victor, L. *Thomas Young's Autobiographical Sketch*. Proc. American, Philosophical Society. Philadelphia: American Philosophical Society Publishers, 1978. Vol. 122.

Rowell, H. S. *Nature Vol. 88*. New York: Nature Publishing Co. 1912.

Science Digest, Vol. 43. Palm Coast: Family Media Inc., 1958.

Wellcome Foundation Library, London.